Peace Be Upon Ibrahim
Vol. I

A collection of memories from the life of Shaheed Ibrahim Hadi

Translated by
Sayyid Haydar Jamaludeen

Translated from the Persian book *"Salam bar Ibrahim"*
Translated by Sayyid Haydar Jamaludeen
Edited by a group of sincere lovers of the martyrs.
Book cover design by Ahmed Cherri

First edition published in 2018
Second edition published in 2020
ISBN: 978-1-7384949-4-1

In the Name of God,
the Beneficent, the Merciful

بسم رب الشهداء والصديقين

In the Name of the Lord
of the Martyrs and the Righteous

CONTENTS

He is Absolute Love	1
Why Ibrahim Hadi?	4
Biography	6
His Father's Love	8
Halal Sustenance	9
Varzesh-e Bastani	11
The Champion	15
One-Man Volleyball	18
Betting	20
Wrestling	23
The Victor	25
Poorya-ye Vali	27
Defeating the Nafs	29
Yadollah	32
Hawzah of Ayatollah Mujtahidi	33
The Divine Union	35
The Days of the Revolution	36
8th September	39
The Return of Imam Khomeini (ra)	41
Spiritual Elevation	42
The Effect of Words	44
Tending to People	47
Kurdistan	50
The Exemplary Teacher	53
The Head of Sport	56
Praying on Time	57
An Encounter with a Thief	60
The Beginning of the War	61
The Second Appearance	65
The Tasbih of Lady Fatimah (a)	67
Shahrak al-Mahdi	69
The Problem Solver	71
The Shaheed Andarzgu Battalion	72
The Martyrdom of Asghar Vesali	76
A Simple Appearance	77
The Imam Hasan (a) Riverbank	79

The Prisoner	81
The 15th of Sha'ban	83
The Prize	85
Abu Ja'far	87
The Friend	92
Lost at War	93
Only for Allah	95
In the Presence of the Great	97
Ziyarah	99
The Grenade	101
Operation Matla' al-Fajr	102
Miracle of the Adhan	106
The Scarves	111
Sense of Humour	112
The Two Brothers	114
The Pistols	115
Operation Fath ol-Mobin	120
Wounded	124
Recitation	127
The Majlis of Lady Fatimah (a)	130
The Summer of '82	132
The Method of Nurturing	134
Correct Conduct	136
The Tale of the Snake	139
The Pleasure of Allah	140
Sincerity	143
The People's Needs and Allah's Blessings	145
Khums	150
We Love You	151
Operation Zayn al-Abideen (a)	152
The Last Days	156
Fakkeh, the Last Stop	159
Operation Before the Dawn	162
The Kumayl Trench	166
The Bloody Sunset	169
The Peak of Oppression	171
Captivity	174
Separation	176
Searching For the Martyrs	177

Presence	179
Peace be upon Ibrahim	183
The Martyrs are Alive	184
Where Are You Going?!	185
The Memorial Gravestone	187
Endnotes	189

HE IS ABSOLUTE LOVE

This book is not a mere recollection of this martyred hero but also a testament to this man's character who attained the lofty status of martyrdom after great displays of bravery, morals and champion-like behaviour.

Our teenagers and youth are easily impressed by shallow role models in sports or art at a time when they need much more. They find themselves walking the path of life facing such difficult and numerous trials. There are pits dug before every step they take. In a time where wolves lie in ambush dressed in sheep's clothing, reviewing the lives of Ibrahim and others like him become like lights in the darkness of the night, just as our great leader said, "We can find our way with the help of these stars."

Ibrahim graduated from the school of wilayah and he became a teacher of the lessons of sincerity, love and self-sacrifice. He took a sip from the cup of the pool of Kowthar's cupbearer and eventually became one of the cupbearers who would go on to serve the other thirsty people. He learnt how to defeat his nafs[1] from

---

1   Arabic for 'one's whims and desires'

none other than his master Ali (a)[2]. He showed you can do anything without being infallible and even at the peak of freedom you can still be a slave, but a slave who is bound only to Allah.

In history before the advent of Islam [in Iran], an Iranian youth known for his courage, heroism and patriotism stood out from the rest and after its advent, by learning the virtues of generosity, purity, chastity, truthfulness, piety and martyrdom from the Ahlulbayt (ams), the name of this youth sparkled across the sky of excellence to such an extent that even the arrogant powers of the world admitted to his greatness and praised him. The era of the Islamic Revolution and the Holy Defence is a witness to these claims.

Reviewing the state of the Iranian youth in that day and age under the guidance of a wise and elderly leader is like looking out at the ocean. Some merely enjoy themselves by watching its grandeur and splendour. Others take a step further and swim in this ocean while looking out in delight. Some are not even content with this; they dive into the ocean to reach the seabed and search for pearls and jewels among the rocks. Without a doubt, the jewels and pearls discovered in the ocean of the Holy Defence are plentiful and they are a source of pride for this honourable country and our religion that we hold dear. Many of these jewels remain hidden from us at the bottom of the ocean. Every now and then, Allah showers His mercy upon us and reveals a pearl from the ocean to inform us about how boundless it really is!

What have we done and what will we do in the future? Will we make these mortals that are envious of the immortals our role models, or worse, will we end up losing our humanity completely?! Creatures resembling humans following another religion and from another hometown have attacked with beautiful and heroic

---

[2] (a) means *alayhis salam* (peace be upon him), (ra) means *rahmatullah alayh* (Allah's mercy be upon him), (s) means *sallallahu alayhi wa alihi wa sallam* (peace be upon him and his progeny), (aj) means *ajjalallahu farajah* (may Allah hasten his reappearance) and (ams) means *alayhim al-salam* (peace be upon them)

disguises while controlling the waves of the media. They have come to rob our youth of their enthusiasm and religion!

These youth of Iran have their roots firmly planted in the soil of wilayah, watered by the pure springs of tears for Imam Husayn (a), tears which have been flowing through their veins and incorporated in them alongside the milk of their mothers. They bear the seals of the benevolence of Abbas (a) and the love of our mother Fatimah (a) on their hearts. Our youth always strive for virtuousness and search for those who can help them achieve this. Their honesty and permanent love remain unshaken and are firmly instilled in them. At times, the enemy is successful in misguiding them. However, one month of Muharram is enough to awaken their existence and conscience to hinder the enemy's plots. Despite their weakness, their roots are well-founded and earthbound. They are looking for an Ibrahim who can destroy the idols of their souls with his axe.

Let's continue. Our goal for praising the Iranian youth in this manner was not to flatter them nor is it an exaggeration, but rather it was to show that Shaheed[3] Ibrahim Hadi was one of these jewels of the ocean. Gathering these memories from his life took years, memories which were narrated by his friends who, just like himself, are unknown, making this task so difficult. However, like the poet, Khajeh Hafez Shirazi once said:

> *The route to the beloved's home is riddled with danger,*
> *The first condition is that you must be infatuated with the beloved.*

We interviewed tens of his friends and family members for the pages of this golden book about this unknown mystic, compassionate teacher, religious youth from the country of Iran and unrivalled champion to be prepared. By the grace of Allah and with the help of Imam Mahdi (aj), we pray this book will become a

---

[3] Meaning 'martyr'

source of inspiration and education for you, dear reader.

In conclusion, we would like to thank everyone who strived to gather this collection of memories and we to reading your thoughts, suggestions and constructive criticisms so that we can try and better introduce the martyrs of this nation. We must keep in mind that our efforts in narrating the stories of the martyrs or compiling books about them are nothing in comparison to their efforts to protect our religion and honour, fulfilling their religious duty in this manner.

WHY IBRAHIM HADI?

Narrator: The Shaheed Ibrahim Hadi Cultural Organisation

It was summer 2007 and I was praying Maghrib and Isha with the congregation in Amin ad-Dowlah Mosque. Most of the people praying were either scholars or intellectuals. I was praying on the right side of the second line of the congregation. Once I finished praying Maghrib, I noticed with complete surprise as I looked around that everywhere except the mosque was flooded as if it was an island in the middle of the ocean!

The imam of the congregation was a luminous elderly man with a white turban. He stood up and started to address the people. I asked the old man next to me if he recognised the imam and he told me, "He's Shaykh Mohammad Hosein Zahed, the teacher of Ayatollah Haqshenas and Mojtahedi." I had heard a lot about the spiritual grandeur and excellence of Shaykh Hosein Zahed so I listened carefully to what he had to say.

Everyone was silent, their attention towards him. He started talking about mysticism and akhlaq[4], "My brothers, the people know us as the legends of mysticism and akhlaq, but the true legends of practical akhlaq and mysticism are these people." He then picked up a picture. I stretched my neck to have a good look. It was a photo of a man with a long beard wearing a brown sweater. After looking at the photo carefully, I realised I recognised the person in the photo. I had seen his face many times before. I had no doubt that it was him. It was Ibrahim, Ibrahim Hadi!

I found his speech strange. How could Shaykh Hosein Zahed, the great teacher of akhlaq and mysticism and taught many great scholars, consider himself a student of Ibrahim?! How could he name Ibrahim as his teacher in practical akhlaq?! Suddenly, I realised, "Shaykh Hosein Zahed... he died a few years ago!"

I woke up in shock. It was three o'clock in the morning on the 11th of August 2007, which coincided with the 27th of Rajab, the day the Holy Prophet (s) was elected by Allah as His messenger. This dream felt like a true dream and it sent shivers down my spine. I found a piece of paper and wrote down whatever I saw and heard. After that, I couldn't fall back asleep. I kept thinking about everything I had heard about Ibrahim Hadi.

Another night I will never forget was the last night of the holy month of Ramadan in 1994, which I spent at the al-Shuhada Mosque. My friends from the war and I went to Shaheed Ibrahim Hadi's house to attend the memorial in remembrance of his late mother. His house was behind the mosque on Shaheed Muwafeq Road. Haj Hosein Allah-Karam started to speak about Shaheed Hadi. The memories he narrated were mesmerising. I had never heard of anyone greater than him in my whole life.

That night, I felt as if Allah's mercy had been showered upon

---

Akhlaq is good manners, morals and conduct

me. I didn't take part in the war and at the time of his martyrdom, I was only seven years old, but Allah wanted me to attend that gathering so that I could learn more about one of His sincere servants. I thought about these memories for years. I couldn't believe that a soldier could show such heroic behaviour and then the people forget about him! What was stranger was that Allah wanted him to remain unknown and after all these years, neither his body was recovered nor was he mentioned at all! I would make sure to mention him to all my classmates during our lessons.

There was still some time left until Fajr, but I didn't feel sleepy. I wanted to find out why Shaykh Hosein Zahed would take Ibrahim as his role model for practical akhlaq. The next day, I visited Shaykh Hosein Zahed's grave in Ibn-e Babawayh Cemetery. When I saw his face on his grave, I had no doubt that my dream was real. I had no doubt that we should not look for mystics in the mountains or monasteries, rather, the real mystics are living among and with us.

That day, I contacted one of Shaheed Hadi's friends and I asked him for the details of all of Shaheed Hadi's close ones. I had made my decision: I must get to know Shaheed Hadi better and I asked Allah for the ability to do that. Maybe this was a duty that Allah had placed on our shoulders so that we could introduce one of His sincere servants to the world.

BIOGRAPHY

Ibrahim was born on the 21st of April 1957 on Shaheed Ayatollah Sa'eedi Street, close to Khorasan Square. He was the fourth child of his family, but his father Mashhadi Mohammad Hosein had a special place in his heart for him. Similarly, Ibrahim also had a special love and respect for his father. He managed to bring up his children in the best possible manner just from the income of a small newsagent. Ibrahim was orphaned when he was a teenager and from that day on, he carried himself around like a man. He attended Taleqani Primary School, Abu Reyhan High School and Kareem Khan Zand High School.

In 1976, he earned a diploma in literature. As he was finishing high school, he was also doing extra-curricular studies. Participating in the Islamic Unity Youth Organisation's programmes and studying under esteemed scholars such as Allamah Mohammad Taqi Jafri shaped his personality and determined how he would go on to live his life. During the Islamic Revolution in Iran, he displayed extreme bravery and courage.

In addition to his studies, Ibrahim would also work in the bazaar of Tehran. After the Revolution, he started working for the Sports Department and then he was transferred to the Education and Training Department. During this period, Ibrahim worked selflessly to nurture the children of his homeland.

He loved sports. He started doing *Varzesh-e Bastani*[5] or the sport of champions as known in Iranian culture. He was unrivalled in volleyball or wrestling. He would never pass up a challenge and would stand steadfast.

The tall peaks of the Bazi-Deraz Mountain Range, Gilan-e Gharb and the scorching plains of the South all bear witness to his valour and courage. His heroics in these provinces are kept alive by his comrades.

He resisted against the Iraqi troops for five days during Operation Before the Dawn[6] with the soldiers of the Hanzaleh and Kumayl Battalions in the besieged trenches of Fakkeh, but they

---

5   A kind of weightlifting done with weights while reciting duas or poems. Normally, the drums are played during exercise.

6   عملیات والفجر مقدماتی

refused to surrender. Eventually, after sending the other soldiers back, he returned to his Lord alone on the 11th of February[7] 1983. Nobody saw him or his body after that. He had asked Allah for his body to be lost because having no grave is a characteristic of those loved by Allah. Allah accepted his prayer; Ibrahim has remained unknown, alone and estranged in the land of Fakkeh to be a guiding light for those who wish to see.

HIS FATHER'S LOVE

Narrator: Reza Hadi (The martyr's brother)

We used to live in a small rented house close to Khorasan Square in Tehran. It was almost the end of April 1957. Our father was in good spirits as Allah had granted him a son. He would constantly thank Allah for this blessing. Even though we were already three brothers and one sister, our father was delighted with this baby. He had every right to be; after all, he was a very cute baby. He named the new-born Ibrahim after the great prophet who was a symbol of patience and a champion of trust in Allah and Tawhid[8]. Ibrahim truly deserved this name.

Whenever friends and family would visit, they would exclaim, "Hosein Agha[9], you have three other sons, why are you so glad over this child?!" and our father would reply calmly, "I have a good feeling about this child. I'm sure that my Ibrahim will become a good servant of Allah and he will revive my name," and truly, he spoke the truth.

---

7   22nd of Bahman (day of the success of the Revolution)
8   Belief in the oneness of Allah
9   Agha is a term used in Iran for men, and is used as a sign of respect

His love for Ibrahim was a strange kind of love. Although after Ibrahim, Allah gave our family one more brother and sister, his love for Ibrahim never diminished.

Ibrahim used to attend Taleqani Primary School on Zeeba Street. He had great akhlaq and even in primary school, he never abandoned his prayers. He said to his friend in primary school once, "My father is a very good person. He has seen Imam Mahdi (aj) in his dream a few times. Also, once he really wanted to go to Karbala to visit the shrines and he saw in his dream that Hazrat Abbas (a) had come to visit and speak with him." In his last year of primary school, he told his friends, "My dad says that Imam Khomeini is a very good person and the Shah[10] has exiled him for many years. My dad even says that everyone must do what he says because his orders are the orders of Imam Mahdi (aj)," but his friends told him, "Ibrahim, don't say these things ever again because if any of the teachers hear you, they'll expel you." Perhaps Ibrahim's friends found these things a little strange, but he had a staunch belief in his father's words.

HALAL SUSTENANCE

Narrator: The martyr's sister

Prophet Muhammad (s) said, "Bring up your children well otherwise anyone can make your child disobedient."[11] For this reason, our father paid a lot of attention to how he brought us up. Our father was a very God-wary man; he would go to the mosque,

---

10   The king of Iran
11   Nahj al-Fasahah, saying 370

attend lectures regularly and give a lot of importance to halal[12] sustenance. He knew well that the Prophet (s) had said, "Worship has ten parts and nine parts of that are gaining halal sustenance."[13] For this reason, when a few people started to harass him and were not allowing him to earn *halal* income from his shop, he decided to sell the shop which he had inherited from his father and started working at a sugar cube factory. He worked as a labourer there and from morning until evening, he would stand in front of the burning furnace until he was able to buy a small house.

Ibrahim said several times, "The main reason my father was able to bring up good children was the suffering and sacrifice he had to go through to earn halal sustenance for us." He would say, reminiscing over his childhood, "My father would make me memorise the Qur'an. He would always take me to the mosque. We would normally go to the mosque where Ayatollah Noori would lead prayers. There was a religious committee by the name of The Ali Asghar Committee there. My father had the honour of volunteering for them."

I remember that one day, Ibrahim did something that made our father angry and he told Ibrahim to leave the house and not come back until the evening. Ibrahim left and did not come back until the evening. The whole family was worried about what he was going to eat for lunch, but we did not say anything to our father. Ibrahim returned at night and said *salaam*[14] respectfully to everyone. I asked him straight away if he had eaten anything for lunch. Our father tried to show him that he was still angry while he was waiting for an answer. Ibrahim said calm and quiet, "I was walking down the road when I saw an old lady who had bought a lot of groceries but she didn't know how to take them home, so I went and helped her. She was very grateful and gave me a five

---

[12] A word used for 'permissible' in Islam
[13] Bihar al-Anwar, vol. 103, p. 7 (العبادة عشرة أجزاء تسعة أجزاء في طلب الحلال)
[14] Meaning 'peace' used as a greeting.

rial coin. I didn't want to accept it, but she insisted. I was sure that this money was halal because I had worked for it. At noon, I bought some bread with that money and ate it for lunch." When our father heard his story, he smiled. He was pleased that Ibrahim had learnt a very valuable lesson from him about the importance of halal sustenance.

The friendship between Ibrahim and his father was more than just the mere father-son relationship. There was a strange love between these two and this helped Ibrahim's personality to develop fruitfully, but this friendship was not destined to last long. Ibrahim was only a teenager when he lost his father's support. One painful evening, the heavy shadow of being an orphan was cast upon him. From then on he carried on with his life, never letting his head drop. That year, many of his friends and family advised him to start doing sports and he took their advice.

VARZESH-E BASTANI

Narrator: Some of the martyr's friends

Ibrahim started to get involved in *Varzesh-e Bastani* around the time he started high school. At nights, he would go to Haj Hasan's gym[15]. Haj Hasan Tavakkol, better known as Haj Hasan Najjar, was a pious mystic who owned a gym close to Abu Reyhan High School. Ibrahim started to attend this athletic and spiritual environment. Haj Hasan would start the exercise with a few verses of the Holy Qur'an and then he would narrate a saying from one of the Infallibles (ams) and translate it. Most of the time,

---

15   Whenever we speak of a gym, we are talking of an Iranian gym in which people would normally do Varzesh-e Bastani.

he would send Ibrahim to the ring who would normally recite one chapter of the Qur'an, Dua Tawassul[16] or a poem that had some relevance to the Ahlulbayt (ams) during one round of exercise.

One of the important things that they would do in this gym was whenever their exercise would continue until Maghrib, they would stop and pray behind Haj Hasan in the ring. This way, Haj Hasan would teach the youth about faith and akhlaq alongside sport during the toxic era before the Revolution.

I will never forget what happened one night. The youth were busy changing their clothes after exercise and saying goodbye to each other when suddenly, a man burst into the gym with a small child in his arms. He cried shakily, "Haj Hasan, help me! My child is sick, and the doctors have said that he cannot be cured. I'm losing him, you're a holy man, please pray for him, I beg you!" and then he started crying. Ibrahim stood up, told the others to change their clothes and go to the ring and then he went to the ring himself. He did one more round of exercise and read Dua Tawassul with the others. After that, they prayed for the child from the bottom of their hearts as the man was sitting in the corner with his child, crying.

Two weeks later, Haj Hasan announced after exercise, "On Friday, we have all been invited for lunch!" I asked him where and he replied, "The man who came with his sick child has invited us. Alhamdulillah[17], his child has been cured. The doctors said that he has become better and so, he has invited us to thank us." I looked back at Ibrahim. He was getting ready as if he hadn't heard anything. I have no doubt that the child was cured only because of the Dua Tawassul Ibrahim recited.

---

16 A supplication in which one seeks intercession from the Infallibles (ams) and is recited generally on Tuesday nights or whenever someone has a problem which requires immediate relief.

17 Meaning 'all praise is to Allah'

I often saw that Ibrahim would make friends with people that neither looked religious nor had anything to do with religion. He would bring them to exercise and after a while, he would take them to the mosque and lectures.

One of the people he made friends with was much worse than the rest. He would always talk about drinking alcohol and doing inappropriate things. He didn't know anything about religion. He didn't show any importance to prayers, fasting or anything else for that matter. He would even boast, "Until now, I have never been to a lecture or a religious gathering." Once, I asked Ibrahim, "Who are these people that you're always spending time with?" He asked with complete surprise, "Why, what happened?" I told him, "Last night, the person you brought with you to the lecture sat next to me. The Shaykh was speaking about the oppression done upon Imam Husayn (a) and the things Yazid did to him. This friend of yours was listening with his full attention and was getting angry. When they turned the lights off, instead of crying, he started swearing at Yazid!" Ibrahim was listening to what I was saying and suddenly, he broke out in laughter. He then said, "No problem, this person has never been to a lecture neither has he ever cried for Imam Husayn (a). I assure you that when he makes a relationship with Imam Husayn (a), he will change but these people will only become religious if we help them."

That youth became such good friends with Ibrahim that he gave up all the bad acts he used to do and became one of our pious bodybuilders. A few months later during Nowruz[18], I saw that the same youth. He had brought a box of cakes and was giving them out, saying, "My friends, I'm indebted to you. I am indebted to you, Ibrahim. I'm very thankful to Allah. If I didn't get to know you, God knows where I would have been!"

I spent the entire way home thinking about Ibrahim's behaviour. I found it astonishing how he managed to bring these

---

18 Iranian New Year

friends to exercise and then from there, he would take them to the mosque and the religious programmes. In his own words, he would take them and seat them on Imam Husayn (a)'s lap. He reminded me of the Prophet (s)'s saying as he said to Imam Ali (a), "Oh Ali (a), guiding one person [to the right path] is greater than anything the sun shines upon."[19]

Sometimes, the youth who would normally work out at Haj Hassan's gym would get together as a group and go and work out at a different gym. One night during the Holy Month of Ramadan, we went to a gym in Karaj. I will never forget that night. Ibrahim was reciting poems and *duas*[20] whilst exercising. Ibrahim had been doing push-ups in a style of *Varzesh-e Bastani*[21] for quite a while. The groups of people exercising changed often but Ibrahim was still doing push-ups and didn't pay attention to anybody else. There was an old man who was sitting at the top of the platform and watching the youth exercise. He came to me, pointed at Ibrahim and asked worriedly who he was. I asked the reason and he replied, *"When I entered, he was doing push-ups. I counted his push-ups with my rosary, and I have completed seven of my rosaries. This means that he has done seven hundred push-ups! Please take him out of the ring; he is going to fall sick!"* When we finished exercising, Ibrahim came out of the ring as if nothing happened. He didn't feel tired at all. It was as if he hadn't been doing push-ups for four hours!

Of course, Ibrahim would exercise to become stronger. He would always say, "To serve Allah and His servants, one must have a strong body." He would ask Allah to strengthen his body for His service.

19	Bihar al-Anwar, vol. 5, pg. 28
20	Arabic for 'supplication'
21	A sort of push-up where one goes up and down according to the beat of the drum. This is normally done in groups.

Ibrahim bought a pair of extremely heavy weights for himself. Everyone was talking about him, saying how strong he is. After a while, he stopped lifting in front of the other youth who would come to the gym. He said, "These things cause us to become proud. People only look for the person who is stronger than the rest. If I keep doing these exercises in front of others, my friends will start to get upset [because no one will pay attention to them]. I have thought about my actions and realised I was making a mistake."

When he was the coach, he would quickly change the exercise to a different one whenever would see that one of the participants was feeling tired and wasn't able to exercise properly.

Ibrahim only showed his true strength the day Sayyid Hosein Tahami, one of Haj Hasan's friends, came to the gym and exercised with the youth.

THE CHAMPION
Narrator: Hosein Allah-Karam

Sayyid Hosein Tahami[22] came to our gym and exercised with the youth. Even though he hadn't competed for a while, he still had a very strong and toned body. After exercising, he said to Haj Hasan, "Is there anyone who would like to wrestle with me, Haji?" Haj Hasan looked at us and told Ibrahim to go to the ring. The rules of championship wrestling state that if your opponent falls, he loses. They started wrestling with everybody watching. They were wrestling for a long period of time but neither of them managed to floor the other. They both put a lot of pressure on each other, but neither was able to make the other fall. Hence, there was no winner. After the match, Sayyid Hosein applauded Ibrahim loudly, saying, "Well done, well done. What a brave young man! Well done

---

22 World wrestling champion in 1964

champion!"

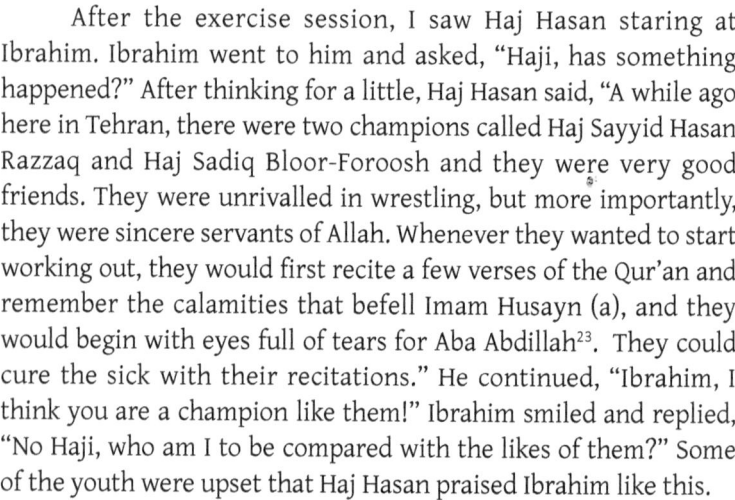

After the exercise session, I saw Haj Hasan staring at Ibrahim. Ibrahim went to him and asked, "Haji, has something happened?" After thinking for a little, Haj Hasan said, "A while ago here in Tehran, there were two champions called Haj Sayyid Hasan Razzaq and Haj Sadiq Bloor-Foroosh and they were very good friends. They were unrivalled in wrestling, but more importantly, they were sincere servants of Allah. Whenever they wanted to start working out, they would first recite a few verses of the Qur'an and remember the calamities that befell Imam Husayn (a), and they would begin with eyes full of tears for Aba Abdillah[23]. They could cure the sick with their recitations." He continued, "Ibrahim, I think you are a champion like them!" Ibrahim smiled and replied, "No Haji, who am I to be compared with the likes of them?" Some of the youth were upset that Haj Hasan praised Ibrahim like this.

The next day, five wrestling champions from one of the gyms in Tehran came to our gym. They suggested that our two gyms wrestle after working out, and we agreed. We all accepted Haj Hasan as a referee. After working out, the wrestling began. Of the first four matches played, we won two of them while the guests won the other two. However, the guests started causing problems during the fourth match. They started raising their voices and shouting at Haj Hasan who was becoming very upset. I paid attention to the competition sheet and noticed that the next match was between Ibrahim and one of the guests. They knew Ibrahim well and they were sure they were going to lose, so they started making problems so that they could blame the referee when they lose! Everybody was angry. A few moments passed, and Ibrahim entered the ring. With a smile playing on his lips, he shook the

---

23   A title used for Imam Husayn (a)

players' hands one by one. Everyone slowly calmed down. He then told us that he was not going to wrestle. Everybody was shocked; why would he do that?! He paused for a bit and added calmly, "Our friendship is worth more than this rude behaviour," and he then kissed Haj Hasan's hand. With one Salawat[24], he announced the end of the contest. Perhaps there was no winner that day, but the real champion was Ibrahim. As we were going to change our clothes and leave, Haj Hasan called us over and asked, "Now do you understand why I call Ibrahim a true champion?" We didn't have anything to say. He continued, "Look, my children, being a champion is what you saw today. Today, Ibrahim wrestled with his nafs and came out victorious. Today, Ibrahim didn't wrestle with them for the sake of Allah and by doing so he managed to prevent arguments and bad feelings. My dear ones, being a real champion is what you witnessed today."

We had the pleasure of witnessing these things from Ibrahim until the victory of the Revolution. After that, most of the youth became busy helping the Revolution and they would hardly come to the gym. One day, Ibrahim suggested that we come to the gym at dawn, pray Fajr in congregation and then work out. Everyone thought this was a great idea. We started going to the gym before the adhan[25] every morning, pray Fajr in congregation and then work out. After that, we eat some breakfast and then we would go to work. Ibrahim was happy about this new programme because on one hand, we were still working out and on the other, we were also praying Fajr in congregation. He would always tell us the Prophet (s)'s saying, "Praying Fajr in congregation is more beloved in my eyes than staying up all night praying."

---

24 Sending salutations upon the Prophet (s) and his family
25 The Islamic call to prayer

Once the war began, we were unable to go to the gym as often as we would normally and most of the youth had gone to the warfront. Also, Ibrahim wasn't in Tehran that often either. I remember that one time when he came back to Tehran, he took his weights with him so that he could work out when he went to war, and he even set up exercise sessions there.

Haj Hasan Tavakkol's gym was truly outstanding in developing champions. In addition to Ibrahim, many of the youth from the gym proved their worth to their Lord. They protected their faith with their blood; they were the real champions. The beautiful and spiritual era of Haj Hasan's gym came to an end once the Holy Defence[26] began and the martyrdom of Shaheed Hasan Shahabi (gym owner), Shaheed Asghar Ranjbaran (commander of the Ammar Brigade), and Shaheed Sayyid Salehi, Shaheed Mohammad Shahroudi, Shaheed Ali Khorramdel, Shaheed Hasan Zahedi, Shaheed Sayyid Mohammad Sobhani, Shaheed Sayyid Javad Majdpour, Shaheed Reza Pand, Shaheed Hamdollah Moradi, Shaheed Reza Houryar, Shaheed Majeed Faridvand, Shaheed Qasem Kazemi, Shaheed Ibrahim Hadi and several others, in addition to the valorous fighting of Haj Ali Nasrollah, Mostafa Harandi, Ali Moqaddam and also the passing of Haj Hasan Tavakkol meant that the time for exercise was finally over. A while later, the gym was transformed into a block of flats and this meant that all that was left from our time at the gym was our memories.

ONE-MAN VOLLEYBALL

Narrator: Some of the martyr's friends

Since the beginning of high school, one could easily assume that Ibrahim was good at sports from his toned muscles. During sports classes, he would always play volleyball and none of the other kids

---

26   The name given to the eight-year war between Iran and Baathist Iraq from 1980-88

could beat him. Once, he played on his own against a team of six boys. They only managed to return the ball three times during the whole match! We all watched Ibrahim win, and from that day onwards, he would mostly play volleyball on his own.

On the holidays and weekends, we used to play behind the fire station on 17 Shahrivar Street. Many of the children who would claim to be good at volleyball were not even a worthy opponent for him. As for the best memory of Ibrahim playing volleyball, it goes back to the days of the war in Gilan-e Gharb. There was a volleyball ground there where the soldiers used to play. One day, a few minibuses came to visit the war areas in Gilan-e Gharb. The leader of the group was Agha Davoudi, the head of the Sports Department. Agha Davoudi was Ibrahim's sports teacher in high school and knew him very well. He gave Ibrahim some sports equipment and told him to use it in whichever way he thought fit. He then added, "My friends here have experience in every sport and have come to visit." Ibrahim gave a short speech to the sportsmen and showed them the different places in the city until we reached the volleyball ground. Agha Davoudi said, "A few of the members of our group are part of the Tehran volleyball team. What do you say that we play some volleyball?" The game started at three in the afternoon. Five players including three professional volleyball players stood on one side and Ibrahim stood alone on the other side. There was a large audience and Ibrahim, as usual, came out barefooted wearing an undershirt with his baggy trousers pulled up as per usual. He stood against them and played so well; the audience was awestruck. The game ended after one half with Ibrahim winning by ten points. After the match, the sportsmen took a photo with Ibrahim as a memento. They could not believe an ordinary soldier like himself could play on the level of the best professional players in the world.

One day in the Dokouheh Military Base, I was telling the soldiers how well Ibrahim plays volleyball. One of the soldiers went and brought a ball. He then made two teams and called Ibrahim. He refused to play at first, but after our insistence, he said, "If I must, all of you must be on one side and me alone on the other!" Some of the commanders who were watching the game said after it ended, "We have never laughed so much. Whenever Ibrahim would hit the ball, a few of the boys would run towards the ball, bump into each other and fall over!" Ibrahim won the match by many points.

BETTING

Narrators: Mahdi Faridvand, Saeed Salehtaash

It was 1975. We were playing on a Friday morning when three strangers came and said, "We are from west Tehran. Which one of you is Ibrahim?" Ibrahim introduced himself and they then said, "Let's play for 200 tomans." A few minutes later, the game started. Ibrahim played solo against all three of them, but they still lost. That same day, we went to one of the neighbourhoods in the south of the city. We played for 700 tomans. It was a good game and we won very quickly. They started collecting money from each other to pay us and Ibrahim noticed this. He said quickly, "I will play with one of you, and if you win, we won't take any money." One of them came forward and started playing and to my surprise, Ibrahim played so badly that he lost! They all left happy, but I was angry with Ibrahim and asked him why he did that. He looked at me and replied, "I didn't want to embarrass them. If you put all the money they had together, it wouldn't even amount to 100 tomans!"

The following week, those three people from west Tehran with two more of their friends. They set the bet at 500 tomans. Ibrahim pulled his trousers up and played barefooted. He hit the ball so hard, they couldn't return it! That day as well, Ibrahim won the game by many points.

That night, we went to the mosque with Ibrahim. After

prayers, the scholar delivered a speech about the rules of Islam. He spoke about betting and unlawful money and he said, "The Prophet (s) said, 'Whoever earns money from an unlawful route, he will lose that money in the way of evil and he will face hardship.'"[27] He (s) also said, 'Whoever eats a morsel of unlawful food, forty days of his prayers and supplications are not accepted.'"[28] Ibrahim was listening to what he was saying attentively and after he finished, Ibrahim went up to him and said, "Today, I won 500 tomans from betting on volleyball." He then told him the story and added, "Of course, I gave that money to a needy family!" The scholar replied, "From now on, be careful. Play sports but don't gamble."

The week after, the same people came again but with stronger and more experienced players. They challenged Ibrahim, saying, "This time, let's play over 1,000 tomans!" Ibrahim replied, "I'll play, but I won't bet." They started mocking him, saying things like, "He's scared, he knows he's going to lose, he doesn't have any money," and so on. Ibrahim told them, "Betting is haram[29], if I knew this before, I wouldn't have played with you the last few weeks. I also gave the money to needy families. If you want, we can play without betting," and of course, the game didn't take place.

His friend told us, "Even after Ibrahim told us not to bet anymore, we betted with youth from the Naziabad neighbourhood once and lost a lot of money. Near the end of the game, Ibrahim came. He was so angry at us because we were betting. We didn't have enough money to pay the other team, so when the game finished, Ibrahim came forward, picked up the ball and asked if anyone wanted to play one-on-one with him. One of the players

---

27   Mawa'idh al-Adadiyyah, pg. 25
28   Hukm al-Dhahirah, vol. 1, pg. 317
29   Meaning 'unlawful in Islam'

with the nickname of HQ who was part of the Iranian national team and the captain of the Barq Team came forward and asked arrogantly, "What's the bet on?" Ibrahim replied, "If I win, then you waive the bet you made with our group." The opponent accepted. Ibrahim played so well that everyone became captivated and he beat his opponent with a large advantage. However, he was angry with us for a while after that!"

Not only was Ibrahim good at volleyball, but he was also very good at many other sports. He was a very experienced mountain climber. For three years before the Revolution, he would climb Tajrish Mountain every Friday morning with some of the people from the gym. They would pray Fajr at Imamzadeh[30] Saleh's shrine and then run up the mountain. They would eat breakfast there and then come back down. I will never forget what happened one time. Ibrahim was practising for wrestling and wanted to strengthen his legs, so he carried one of his friends on his back from the bottom all the way to the top of the mountain! He would do mountain climbing in Darband and Kulakchal[31] every week until the Revolution succeeded.

Ibrahim was a good football player and was very experienced in table tennis. He knew how to play with two paddles at the same time and was an unbeaten champion.

---

30   Farsi for 'son of Imam'
31   Boroughs in Tehran

WRESTLING

Narrators: The martyr's brothers

After doing *Varzesh-e Bastani* for a while, Ibrahim followed Haj Hasan's advice and started wrestling. He signed up at the Abu Moslem Wrestling Gym and he was placed in the 53kg weight class. Ibrahim's managers were Agha Mohammadi and Agha Gouderzi, two experienced sportsmen. Agha Mohammadi liked Ibrahim due to his good manners and behaviour and Agha Gouderzi taught him the art of wrestling well. He would always say, "This boy is very calm but when he wrestles, he can attack you like a leopard because he's tall and he has long arms. He won't stop attacking until he wins." For this reason, he gave him the nickname 'The Lying Leopard'. He used to always say, "One day, you'll see this boy in the international championships, I assure you!"

Around the beginning of the 70s, Ibrahim took part in the Tehran Teenage Championship and he defeated all his opponents with ease. He was only fifteen years old when he was chosen to take part in the National Championship. The competition began at the end of October, but Ibrahim didn't show up. As a result, his managers became very angry with him. Afterwards, we found out that the competition was going to take place in the crown prince's presence, and he was going to give the medals during the award ceremony. For this reason, Ibrahim didn't take part in the competition.

The following year, Ibrahim took part in the Academy Championship and won first place. In the same year, he also took part in the 62-kilogram class of the Tehran Wrestling Gym Championships.

When he wanted to enter the Academy Championship the following year, he learnt that his best friend was taking part in the same competition as he was i.e. the 68-kilogram class. Therefore, Ibrahim decided to compete in one weight class higher and entered the 74-kilogram class competition. That year,

Ibrahim's performance stood out and he won the first place of the 74-kilograms class in Academy Championship at the young age of eighteen.

He knew how to use his legs, the right kinds of strategies and his long arms well, and this was the reason why he became a perfect wrestler.

One day, Ibrahim left home with his wrestling equipment at dawn, so my brother and I followed him wherever he went until he got to the 7 Teer Hall. We followed him inside and sat among the audience. There were many people in the hall. An hour later, the wrestling started. Ibrahim wrestled in a few rounds and he won all of them. When he saw us cheering for him amongst the audience, he came up to us angrily and asked us why we had followed him. We replied, "No reason. We just came to see where you were going." He exclaimed, "What do you mean?! You shouldn't be here. Get up and go home." I asked with surprise what had happened, and he repeated, "You shouldn't stay here. Get up, let's go home." As soon as we were about to leave, the speakers boomed, "74-kilogram semi-final, Agha Hadi versus Agha Tehrani!" Ibrahim looked at the ring and then looked back to us. He paused for a few moments and then he went to the ring while we were cheering for him. His manager was constantly shouting and telling Ibrahim what to do. However, Ibrahim was only defending and was constantly throwing glances in our direction. His manager was getting angry and yelled, "Ibrahim, what are you doing?! Hit him already!" With one graceful movement, Ibrahim picked his opponent up, spun him in the air and then threw him down onto the cushions. Ibrahim left the ring before the match finished.

That day, Ibrahim was very angry with us. I thought he was annoyed because we followed him. As we were speaking on the way home, he said, "One must do exercise to become strong, not to win. I only enter these competitions to learn new wrestling techniques. Otherwise, there's no other reason for me to enter these competitions." I asked, "But is it bad for someone to want to become famous and be a champion?" He paused for a bit and then told me, "Not everybody can be famous. Becoming a human is more important than becoming famous." That day, Ibrahim had reached the final, but he came back home with us before competing in the final. He showed us in action that ranks and position had no value in his eyes. Ibrahim would always repeat the famous saying of Imam Khomeini (ra), "Sport must not be the aim in one's life."

THE VICTOR

Narrator: Hosein Allah-Karam

Ibrahim was defeating his opponents one after the other in the 74-kilogram class of the Gym Championship until he reached the semi-finals. He had trained well that year and beaten all his opponents with ease. If he wrestled properly, I think he would have won the competition. However, in the semi-finals, he wrestled very poorly and eventually, he forfeited the competition, settling for third place. A few years later, the person who defeated Ibrahim in the semi-finals came to visit him. He was talking to us about the memories he shared with Ibrahim and we were all listening. He then started to talk about how he got to know Ibrahim, "Our friendship goes back to the semi-finals of the 74-kilogram class of the Gym Championship when I fought Ibrahim," but whenever he wanted to tell the story, Ibrahim would change the subject. Eventually, the story remained untold.

The next day, I saw him again and I asked him to tell me the story. He took a deep breath and told me, "That year, I was drawn against Ibrahim in the semi-finals, but one of my legs was badly hurt. Even though I didn't know Ibrahim properly, I said to him, 'This foot of mine is injured, please try not to hurt it even more.' Ibrahim replied, 'Sure, don't worry, my brother!' I had seen him wrestle before and I knew that he was an expert in wrestling. Even though Ibrahim's wrestling style depended on attacking the opponent's leg, he didn't even come close to it. However, at the peak of cowardice, I picked him up and threw him on the cushions. I was overjoyed to have advanced on to the final. Ibrahim, who could have easily defeated me and won the tournament that year, surprisingly didn't." He continued, "Of course, I think he let me win on purpose. He wasn't even sad that he had lost, because winning meant something else to him. However, I was happy. Even happier because my opponent in the final was one of the people from my neighbourhood. I thought everybody had the same principles and kindness of Ibrahim but in the final, even though I had mentioned to my friend that my leg was injured, his first move was to grab my leg, pick me up and throw me down. That year, I came second and Ibrahim third, but I had no doubt that Ibrahim deserved to be the champion that year. From then onwards, he and I have been good friends. I have since also seen some wonderful things that he has done. I thank Allah for blessing me with such a great friend." When our conversation ended, I bade farewell and we went our own ways. All the way home, I was thinking about what he had told me.

This reminds me of something I saw written on the wall of the army base in Gilan-e Gharb. There was a small sentence written about every soldier on that wall. One of the soldiers had written, "Ibrahim Hadi is a soldier with the qualities of Poorya-ye Vali[32]."

---

32   An Iranian wrestler who was known for his generosity, kindness and morals

POORYA-YE VALI

Narrator: Eeraj Geraei

It was the 1976 Gym Championship. The winner of this contest would win a cash prize and would also be chosen for the national team. Ibrahim was at the peak of fitness and whoever saw him fight once would agree. His managers claimed that no one could beat Ibrahim in the 74-kilogram class that year. The competition began and Ibrahim was defeating his opponents one after the other with ease. He reached the semi-finals after winning four matches. He would either win by throwing the opponent on the cushions or with a big score difference. I said to my friends, "I'm telling you, a wrestler from our gym is going to be chosen for the national team this year."

In the semi-final, even though his opponent was well-built and experienced, and their fight took long, Ibrahim defeated him and marched on to the final. His final opponent was a person called Mahmoud K. who had won the International Army Wrestling Championship earlier that year. Before the final, I went to Ibrahim's dressing room and told him, "I have seen your opponent wrestle before and he is not that good, but Ibrahim, I beg you, please pay attention. Wrestle well, I'm sure that this year you're going to be picked for the national team." His manager gave him his last advice while he was tying his laces and then sent him into the ring. I quickly found a space in the audience and sat down. The referee had not arrived yet, so Ibrahim went forward, said salaam with a smile and shook his opponent's hand. His opponent said something which I couldn't hear but Ibrahim was nodding. He then pointed to someone in the stands. I looked over to where he was pointing, and I saw an old lady sitting alone at the top of the stands doing *dhikr*[33] on a rosary. I didn't understand what had been said or what happened, but Ibrahim started the match very poorly

---

[33] Praising Allah

and was constantly defending. Ibrahim's helpless manager was shouting so much, he lost his voice! It was as if Ibrahim couldn't hear his manager and he was merely wasting time. Ibrahim's rival was afraid to start at the beginning. However, he found the courage to attack slowly and started being more offensive. Ibrahim was also defending very well. The referee gave him his first strike and then his second and finally, Ibrahim was given the third strike and his opponent was named the champion of the 74-kilo class. When the referee raised his opponent's hand, Ibrahim was happy as if he had won himself! The two wrestlers then hugged each other. Ibrahim's opponent bent over and kissed Ibrahim's hand, crying out of joy.

As both were leaving the hall, I flew down from the stands towards Ibrahim furiously. I shouted at him, "What kind of wrestling was that?!" I was so angry, I punched him in the arm and yelled, "If you don't want to wrestle, don't hold us back either!" Ibrahim told me very calmly and with a smile to not be so greedy. He then rushed off to his dressing room, changed his clothes and left. I was so angry, I punched the walls and doors and sat in a corner for half an hour. I waited until I calmed down and then I left.

As I was leaving the hall, I noticed that it was still very busy outside. Ibrahim's opponent was standing there with his entire family and many of his friends who were all extremely happy. All of a sudden, he called me over and asked if I was Ibrahim's friend. I asked him bitterly what he wanted, and he replied, "Your friend is so chivalrous. Before the match, I said to Ibrahim, 'I have no doubt that you are going to beat me. but please don't defeat me too badly. My mother and brother are in the stands and if you defeat me badly, I will lose my face in front of them.'" Your friend went one step further. You don't know how happy my mother is right now." He then started crying and continued, "I have just got married and I needed the cash prize, you don't understand how happy I am." I was lost for words. I stayed silent for a bit and looked at him. I had only just understood then what had happened. I then said, "If I was in his place, after all the difficult practice, I wouldn't have done that. Doing these kinds of things is only what great people do." I bade farewell to the youth and took a glance at his mother who was crying with joy. I then went home. On the way, I thought about what Ibrahim had done. Ignoring such great status and position is not a normal thing to do!

I remembered the story of Poorya-ye Vali. Once, when he realised that his opponent needed to win the competition because the ruler of the city was disturbing him, he lost to his opponent on purpose. I recalled how much Ibrahim practised for this competition, the smile of that old lady, and the happiness of the young man. Suddenly, my eyes welled up with tears; Ibrahim was truly a great man!

DEFEATING THE NAFS

Narrators: Some of the martyr's friends

Heavy rains fell on Tehran and 17 Shahrivar Street was flooded. A few old men wanted to cross the road, but they couldn't find a way. When Ibrahim saw them, he pulled his trousers up and carried them on his back to the other side of the road one after the other.

Ibrahim would do these things often. His aim for doing them was nothing but to defeat his nafs. Another difficult test for him was when his friends would start to praise him for these acts!

One summer afternoon, we were walking with Ibrahim when we walked past some children playing football. As we were passing by, one of the boys kicked the ball and it hit Ibrahim's face so hard that he almost fell over and his face turned very red. I was infuriated, so I looked at the children and they all started to run away so that we wouldn't hit them. Ibrahim put his hand in his bag and pulled out a small plastic bag of walnuts. He shouted, "Where are you going, kids?! Come and take some walnuts!" He then put the bag next to the goalpost and we moved on. On the way home, I asked him why he did that, and he replied, "They were scared and they didn't hit me on purpose," and then he quickly changed the subject, but I knew that only great people act in this manner.

As we were getting ready for practice at the wrestling gym, Ibrahim came. A few minutes later, another one of our friends came and as soon as he came in, he said to Ibrahim, "Ibrahim, you've become so handsome now, what with your style in clothes and your toned physique! On your way, there were two girls following you and they kept talking about you." He then added, "After all, you are wearing a nice shirt and trousers and you are carrying a sports bag. It's obvious you're a bodybuilder!" I looked at Ibrahim. He was deep in thought. He looked sad; it was as if he didn't expect this!

The next time I saw Ibrahim come to the gym, I couldn't stop myself from laughing. He was wearing a long shirt and baggy trousers. Instead of carrying a sports bag, he had put his equipment in a plastic bag and from that day on, this is how he would come to the gym. The youth used to ask, "What kind of a person are you!? We come to the gym to build a bodybuilder's physique and then we wear tight clothes, so why do you come in these clothes despite your toned body?!" but he didn't pay attention to what they were saying. He would advise his friends, "If exercise is for Allah, then it is worship, but if you have other intentions, you are at loss!"

We were playing on the football field when I saw Ibrahim standing beside the stands. I ran over to him. I said salaam and then cheerfully asked why he had come. He held up the magazine he was holding in his hands and told me that they had printed my picture in the magazine. I was so happy, I felt I was going to fly. I went forward and tried to take the magazine out of his hands, but he put the magazine behind his back and told me that I could only see it on one condition. I replied, "I accept your condition, whatever it is." He repeated, "You'll do anything I say?" I replied, "Yeah, man, I accept." He handed me the magazine. On the front page, there was a large, full-page photo of me. One the side, it said, 'The next big thing in football!' The article was full of praise for me. I sat next to the stands and read the article again. I flicked the pages a bit and said to Ibrahim, "Thank you so much. You've made me so happy. By the way, what was your condition?" He calmly asked, "Are you sure that you will accept whatever I tell you?" I said yes. He paused for a bit and then told me not to play football anymore. I was taken aback. After a short silence, I exclaimed, "What do you mean?! They've only just noticed how good I am!" He replied, "Not that you do not play anymore, but don't play professional football." I asked why, so he came forward, took the magazine out of my hand, showed me my photo and said, "Look at this photo; you are here in sports clothes. Not only you and I have access to this magazine, but the whole country has this magazine, and girls may also see this." He added, "I'm only saying this because you are religious. Otherwise, I wouldn't have told you this. First, strengthen your beliefs and then go into professional football." He then said, "I have to be somewhere," bade farewell and left. I was left shaken. I sat down and thought of the things that Ibrahim had said. I didn't expect to hear something like this from a fun and playful person like him. I understood his words a few years later when I saw people who were regulars at the mosque and used to pray become misguided and abandon prayers in the pursuit of professional sports.

YADOLLAH

Narrator: Sayyid Abolfazl Kazemi

Ibrahim was working in one of the shops in the bazaar. One day, I saw him doing something very surprising; he was carrying two large boxes on his shoulder which he put down in front of a shop. When he had finished the delivery, I went up to him and said salaam. I then told him, "Ibrahim, this work does not suit you. This is the work of an average labourer!" He looked at me and said, "There is no imperfection in working, but not having a job is an imperfection. Actually, this job is good for me because it helps me remember that I am nothing and it stops me from becoming proud!" I replied, "It's not good if someone sees you like this, you're a sportsman!" Ibrahim laughed and replied, "Always do that which makes Allah happy, not the people."

I was sitting with a few friends and we were talking about Ibrahim. One of our friends who didn't know Ibrahim took his photo out of my hand and looked at him carefully. He then turned to us and asked, "Are you sure his name is Ibrahim?" We replied, "Yes, why?" He explained, "I used to own a shop in Soltani Bazaar before. Agha Ibrahim would stand at the front of the bazaar two days a week and deliver the people's products to their shops. One day I asked him what his name was, and he said that you can call me Yadollah[34]. After a while, one of my friends came to the bazaar and when he saw Ibrahim, he exclaimed, 'Do you know who that is?!' I said, "No, why?" He replied, 'He is a champion of volleyball

---

34 Meaning 'the hand of Allah'

and wrestling and he is a very pious man. He only does these things to defeat his nafs. Let me tell you this, he is a great person.' After he told me that, I never saw Ibrahim again." What that man had told us made me think. I found this story very strange; fighting your nafs in this manner didn't make any sense!

A while later, I met one of my old friends and we started speaking about what Ibrahim would normally do. He said, "One afternoon before the Revolution, Ibrahim came looking for us. He took me, my brother and two others to a restaurant and bought the best food, salads and drinks for us. It was so delicious to the extent that I had never eaten anything like it before. When we were done eating, Ibrahim asked us how the food was, and I replied, 'It was excellent, thank you very much.' He told us, 'Since the morning, I was delivering people's things to their shops in the bazaar and I earned some money from that. The tastiness of this food is due to the hardship I went through to earn this money.'"

HAWZAH OF AYATOLLAH MUJTAHIDI

Narrator: Eeraj Geraei

During the years leading up to the Revolution, Ibrahim began doing things other than his normal work at the bazaar. Nobody knew nor did he let people know what he was doing, but his behaviour and akhlaq had changed completely. He had become much more spiritual. In the morning, he would carry a black bag and would set off to the bazaar. There were a few books inside that bag.

One day, I saw Ibrahim as I was passing by his road on my motorcycle. I asked him where he was going, and he told me he was going to the bazaar. I asked him to ride with me and on the way to the bazaar, I asked, "I have seen you carrying this bag for a while now. What's inside it?" He replied, "Nothing, just a few books." On the way to the bazaar, he got off at Na'eb as-Saltaneh Road. I was surprised as I knew that he didn't work there, so where could he have gone? I was curious so I followed him until he went inside a mosque. He sat down next to some youth and opened his books. I slowly began to realise he was studying in the *Hawzah*[35]. I left the mosque and asked an old man who was passing by, "Sorry, what's the name of this mosque?" and he told me that it was the Hawzah of Ayatollah Mujtahidi. I looked at my surroundings with surprise as I never thought that Ibrahim was the kind of person to study in the *Hawzah*. On the wall, there was a saying of the Holy Prophet (s), "The skies, earth and the angels ask forgiveness day and night for three groups of people: the scholars, people who seek knowledge and the generous."[36]

That night as we were leaving the gym, I said to him, "So you go to the *Hawzah* and hide it from us, huh?" He turned around abruptly and looked at me surprised, and then he realised that I must have followed him that day. He whispered, "It is a shame for people to spend their lives just eating and sleeping. I'm not an official student. I just attend to gain knowledge and be able to lead my life properly. In the afternoons, I also go to the bazaar and work there, but for now, don't tell anyone that I attend the Hawzah."

Until the Revolution succeeded, Ibrahim's daily routine was as such, but after the Revolution, he was so occupied that he didn't get time to do the things he would normally do before the Revolution.

---

35 Meaning 'Islamic Seminary'

36 Mawa'idh al-Adadiyyah, pg. 111

THE DIVINE UNION
Narrator: Reza Hadi

One afternoon, Ibrahim had just come back from work. As he turned onto our road, he saw our neighbour's son talking to a girl. As soon as the young man saw Ibrahim, he turned around, said goodbye to the girl and they ran away quickly. He couldn't bear to look Ibrahim in the eye.

This happened again a few days later. This time, by the time the young man noticed him, Ibrahim had already gotten very close to them. So, the girl hurried to the other side of the road, leaving the youth to deal with Ibrahim. Ibrahim walked up to him, said salaam and shook his hand. The boy was scared, but Ibrahim was smiling like always. Before he pulled his hand out of the handshake, Ibrahim said calmly, "Look, doing these things in the middle of the road and the neighbourhood will give you a bad reputation. I know you and all your family very well. If you want to get married to this girl, then I will speak to your father and..." The boy interrupted Ibrahim, saying, "No, I beg you, please don't tell my dad. I made a mistake!" Ibrahim replied, "No, that's not what I meant. Look, your father has a large house and you also have a job at his shop. Tonight, I'll speak to your father in the mosque and *Insha'Allah*[37] you'll be able to marry that girl. What else do you want?!" The boy replied with his head lowered in shame, "If my dad finds out, he'll be so angry." Ibrahim replied, "Don't worry about your father, I know him. He's a good and logical person." The boy replied, "I don't know what to say so do your thing," said goodbye and went home.

After prayers that night, Ibrahim spoke to the boy's father. He first spoke about marriage and that if someone is ready to get married and has found someone, he must get married. He added that if anything else happens that results in him falling into sin,

---

[37] Meaning 'if Allah wills'

he must answer to Allah on the Day of Judgement and therefore, the elders must help the youth in this regard. The youth's father supporting everything Ibrahim was saying but when the father realised that he was talking about his son, everything fell through. Ibrahim asked, "Haj Agha, if your son wants to protect himself [from falling into sin], especially in this society, has he done something wrong?" The father thought for a bit and then said no. The day after, Ibrahim's mother spoke with the youth's mother and then the girl's mother.

A month later, Ibrahim was returning from the bazaar at night and he noticed that they were hanging up lights for celebration at the end of our road. A smile of contentment played on Ibrahim's lips; contentment because he was able to turn a sinful friendship into a divine union. This marriage is still steadfast, and the couple owes their happy life together to Ibrahim's perfect solution.

THE DAYS OF THE REVOLUTION
Narrator: Amir Rabiei

Since he was a child, Ibrahim had a special love in his heart for Imam Khomeini (ra). As he grew older, so did this special love, and in the years leading up to the Revolution, this love reached its peak.

It was 1977 and there was still no news of any protests or revolutionary action taking place. One Friday morning, we were returning home from a religious gathering in Jaleh Square (currently Shuhada Square). As we were leaving the square, a few more of our friends joined us. Ibrahim started to tell us about Imam Khomeini (ra) and he suddenly chanted, "Peace be upon Khomeini!" and we followed his lead. A few others joined and chanted with us. We continued doing this until we reached the Shams Square where we noticed a few police cars coming towards us. Ibrahim dispersed the crowd quickly so that we wouldn't be arrested, and we all escaped into the sideroads.

Two weeks later, we were leaving the same Friday morning gathering again. Ibrahim stood in a corner in front of the cinema and shouted, "Peace be upon Khomeini!" The people who had left the gathering joined him and chanted along with us. It was truly a wonderful sight to see. A few minutes later, Ibrahim dispersed the crowd quickly before the agents arrived and we rushed into a taxi towards Khorasan Square. After passing two intersections, we realised that the police had set up a checkpoint and were checking the passengers one by one. A few cars belonging to the SAVAK[38] and around ten agents were lined up on the side of the road. The faces of the agents checking the cars looked familiar to me and at that moment, I realised that they were the same people who accompanied us from the square! I told Ibrahim only to realise he had also noticed them. Before we reached the checkpoint, he got out of the taxi and hurried towards the pavement. The agents realised what was happening. They pointed at Ibrahim and started shouting, "It's him, catch him!" The agents chased Ibrahim down into an alleyway. As the agents were distracted by Ibrahim, I paid the taxi driver, ran to the other side of the road and continued back on home.

I reached home at noon and I hadn't heard anything from Ibrahim. I didn't hear anything from him that night either. I rang some of his friends, but they hadn't heard anything from him. I was very worried. I was sitting in the courtyard of my house around eleven o'clock at night when I heard a noise on the road. I ran to the door to see Ibrahim standing there, smiling. I went forward and hugged him. I didn't know how to express my joy. I asked him how he was. He took a deep breath and replied, "Thank God, as you can see, I am unharmed." I asked if he had eaten dinner and he said no but told me not to worry. I ran into my house and brought bread and some leftovers from earlier that night. We walked down to Ghiyasi Square (currently Shaheed Sa'eedi Square) and he had a little bit to eat. He told me, "At these times, having a strong body helps. I escaped with Allah's help. I managed to get away even though there were many of them." That night we spoke about a lot of things, including the Revolution and Imam Khomeini (ra). We agreed that we would go to Larzadeh Mosque to listen to Ayatollah Chavushi's[39] speeches every night.

One night, Ibrahim and I went to Larzadeh Mosque with three of our friends. Ayatollah Chavushi was extremely fearless and he would say things from the pulpit that others wouldn't even dare to utter. He narrated the saying of Imam Kadhim (a), "A man from the people of Qum will invite the people towards the truth. A group of men will be attracted to him like the pieces of iron to a magnet."[40] These words were very surprising for the people. Suddenly, I heard a large commotion outside. I went to see what was going on and I saw the agents of SAVAK with sticks and batons in their hands hitting everyone indiscriminately. Everybody rushed for the doors and the agents were beating anyone who passed by them. They didn't even have mercy on the women and children. Ibrahim was infuriated. He ran towards the door and started to fight with the agents. All the cowards decided to gang up on Ibrahim and give him a good beating. In these few moments, the route was clear, so the women and children fled to safety. Ibrahim fought them fearlessly. He managed to hit a few of them and then he escaped. We all fled the mosque with him. Later that night, we found out that they had arrested Ayatollah Chavushi and many people had been wounded or martyred. The strikes that Ibrahim had taken to his back gave him back pains for the rest of his life and they also affected his wrestling career.

At the beginning of 1978, all Ibrahim could think about was

---

39 A revolutionary scholar martyred by the hypocrites
40 Bihar al-Anwar, vol. 60, pg. 216

the Revolution and Imam Khomeini (ra). He would courageously distribute leaflets and audiotapes of the Imam (ra). At the beginning of September, he took many of the youth with him to the Gheytariyyeh Barracks to participate in the Eid prayers behind Shaheed Mofatteh. After the prayers, it was announced that there would be a protest towards Jaleh Square on the following Friday.

8TH SEPTEMBER
Narrator: Amir Monjar

It was the morning of the 8th of September[41]. I picked Ibrahim up on my motorcycle and we went to the same religious gathering in Jaleh Square. When the gathering ended, there was a big commotion outside. Around midnight, a curfew had been ordered but most of the people had not been informed. Many soldiers and agents had been stationed around the square, but we could still see many people coming towards us. The agents used loudspeakers and shouted at the crowd to disperse. Ibrahim ran outside then rushed back in and exclaimed, "Amir, come and look at what's happening!" I came out and people were coming towards Jaleh Square from all directions for as far as my eyes could see. The slogan 'peace be upon Khomeini (ra)' was being chanted from every direction, and the slogan of 'down with the Shah' reverberated around the city. The crowds were flooding Jaleh Square. Some were saying that the agents of SAVAK had besieged all four sides of Jaleh Square. A few moments later, something happened that hardly anyone could believe. We started hearing gunshots from all directions even the helicopters were shooting. I quickly went to bring my motorcycle and found a way out through a small alleyway where there were no agents. Ibrahim brought one of the wounded and we returned after taking him to the 3rd Shaban Hospital. By noon, we had been

---

41 Iranian date: 17th of Shahrivar

to the hospital and back around eight times. Almost the whole of Ibrahim's body was drenched in blood [of the wounded].

One of the wounded was lying in a petrol station and the agents were watching him from afar, so nobody dared to help him. Ibrahim wanted to go to his aid, but I stopped him and said, "They are using him as a trap. If you go near him, they will shoot you." Ibrahim looked at me and said, "Would you say the same thing if he was your brother?!" I was lost for words. I just told him to be careful. When the sound of shooting lessened and the agents dropped back a little, Ibrahim seized the opportunity. He quickly crawled onto the road and laid himself down beside the wounded man. He then grabbed his hand and carried him on his back. He came back crawling. He then put him on our motorcycle along with another person and I left with them, leaving Ibrahim behind at his request. On the way back, the agents had closed off that alleyway. The government had tightened the curfew and I had lost Ibrahim. I managed to return home with great difficulty.

I went to Ibrahim's house that afternoon. His mother was incredibly worried as nobody had heard from him. I was extremely worried too. At midnight, I heard that Ibrahim had returned home. I was so relieved. The next day, we went to Behesht-e Zahra[42] to help in the funerals and burials of the martyrs.

After the 8th of September, we would hold nightly gatherings at different people's houses to prepare for the Revolution. For a while, we held them on the roof of Ibrahim's house and then in Mahdi's house and so on. We would address all subjects in these gatherings, especially theological and political matters. We held these gatherings until we received news that Imam Khomeini (ra) was returning to Iran.

---

42   One of the largest cemeteries in the world which most of the people buried within are martyrs

THE RETURN OF IMAM KHOMEINI (RA)

Narrator: Hosein Allah-Karam

It was the beginning of February and after some coordination, we were chosen to be part of Imam Khomeini (ra)'s security team. On the 1st of February, we were armed and sent to the end of Azadi Street[43]. I will never forget when Imam's car entered the road. Just as a moth is attracted to a flame, Ibrahim wanted to get as close as he possibly could to Imam Khomeini (ra)'s car.

As soon as the Imam (ra)'s car had passed, we all went to Behesht-e Zahra together. We were given the duty of guarding the main entrance of Behesht-e Zahra which was on the highway between Qom and Tehran. Ibrahim was standing beside the gate, but his soul was inside, where Imam Khomeini (ra) was delivering his speech. He would say, "The founder of this Revolution has arrived, and we must obey his every command. From today, everything Imam Khomeini (ra) says must be carried out."

Ibrahim wouldn't rest from that day onwards. In Daheh-ye Fajr[44], nobody had heard from Ibrahim for a few days until I saw him on the 9th of February. "Where have you been, Ibrahim?" I asked him, "Your mother is worried about you!" He paused and said, "Over the last few days, my friend and I were trying to identify the bodies of the martyrs because none of the officials were coming to work."

On the eve of the 11th of February[45], Ibrahim and a few of the revolutionary youth from our neighbourhood went to take control

---

43   The road of the airport
44   The ten days between the return of Imam Khomeini (ra) and the success of the Revolution
45   Iranian date: 22nd of Bahman

of the local police station. Once they took control of the 14th Police Station that night, we went around patrolling the neighbourhood. The next morning, the victory of the Islamic Revolution was announced constantly on the radio. Ibrahim worked at Refah School with Amir for a while and then he worked as one of the guards of Imam Khomeini (ra). He then went to Qasr Prison and worked there as a guard for a while. At that time, he would work with the youth of the revolutionary committee, but he didn't officially join them.

SPIRITUAL ELEVATION
Narrators: Jabbar Setoudeh, Hosein Allah-Karam

One thing in common between the lives of all the great scholars is that they would abstain from committing greater sins, and this was beneficial for their speedy spiritual growth. This control of the nafs was mostly concerning one's sexual desires. Allah said about Prophet Yusuf (a)'s story, "Indeed, he who fears Allah and is patient (against his lust and whims), then indeed, Allah does not delay the reward of the gooddoers," which proves that this is a general rule and it is not meant exclusively for Prophet Yusuf (a).

One month after the victory of the Revolution, I noticed that Ibrahim's appearance and physique had become much more attractive. Every day he would come to work in north Tehran wearing a smart suit. One day, I noticed that he was upset and was hardly speaking to anyone. I went up to him and asked him if something had happened. He told me, "No, it's nothing important," but it was clear that something was wrong. I said, "If something has happened, tell me so that I can help you." He paused for a few moments and then whispered, "A girl with bad hijab in this neighbourhood has been disturbing me for a few days now. She said that she won't leave me alone until she has me." I thought for a bit and then, suddenly, I burst out laughing. Ibrahim lifted his head surprised and asked, "Is it funny to you?!" I replied, "Ibrahim, I was thinking about what I had just heard." I took a good look at him then continued, "No wonder she's attracted to you, what with your physique and your style of clothing!" He said, "What do you mean? Do you think that she said these things to me because of my appearance and style?" I smiled and replied, "I have no doubt about it!"

When I saw Ibrahim the next day, I could hardly stop myself from laughing. He came to work without wearing his suit, his head shaved. The day after that, he came in a baggy shirt. His face was messy, and he was wearing Kurdish trousers[46] and slippers. Ibrahim kept doing this until the woman stopped following him.

Attention for detail and accuracy in his work were among some of Ibrahim's traits that distinguished him from his friends. In April 1979, Ibrahim and I went on an operation with some of the youth of the committee. We received intel that someone who was in the military before the Revolution and was on our watchlist had been spotted in an apartment complex. We were given the address and we made our way there in two cars. We entered the apartment and arrested the suspect without any struggle. As we were leaving the building, we noticed that a large crowd had gathered in front of the building to see the suspect. Many of them were residents of that same building.

When Ibrahim saw the crowd, he turned back into the apartment immediately and ordered us to wait. I asked what had happened, but he didn't reply. He untied his scarf from around his

---

46 A kind of baggy trousers worn by the Kurds. Iranians wear these when they want to sleep.

waist and put it around the suspect's face. "What are you doing, Ibrahim?" I asked. As he tied the scarf, he explained, "We have arrested this man based on a report. If that report is not correct, this man's reputation will be tarnished, and he won't be able to live here anymore. Everybody here will look at him as a criminal, but no one will recognise him now. If he is released tomorrow, he won't face any problems with the residents." Nobody recognised the suspect when we left the building. I thought about Ibrahim's attention to detail. He would care so much about the character and reputation of the people.

THE EFFECT OF WORDS

Narrator: Mahdi Faridvand

A few months after the victory of the Revolution, one of my friends said to me, "Go with Ibrahim to the Sports Department tomorrow, Agha Davoudi (the head of the department) wants to see you." The next morning, I got the address and we went to their building. Agha Davoudi, Ibrahim's sports teacher in high school, welcomed us very warmly. We entered the hall with a few others. He said, "You are revolutionary sportsmen, join the organization and get a job here." He said to me and Ibrahim, "I have left the responsibility of inspecting the department for you two." After discussing this with each other for a bit, we accepted the responsibility.

We started working there from the following day and whenever we would face a problem, we would ask Agha Davoudi and he would solve it for us.

I will never forget that one morning; Ibrahim got to the office and asked me what I was doing. I replied, "Nothing much, I am preparing an order of dismissal for someone." He asked who it was for and I told him, "There have been reports from one of the federations that its head comes to work with an unbefitting appearance and style. He also acts inappropriately with the employees, especially the women. There are even claims that he has taken an anti-revolutionary stance. On top of that, his wife doesn't wear hijab!" I was writing the order at that time. I added, "I will also send a copy to the revolutionary committee." Ibrahim asked if he could see the report and I gave him both the report and the order of dismissal. He read the report carefully and asked, "Have you spoken to this man yourself?" I replied, "No, there's no need, everyone knows what kind of person he is." He said, "No, it doesn't work like that. Have you never heard that only a liar accepts everything he's told?" I said, "But the employees of the federation told us-" He interrupted, asking if I had the man's address and I told him I did. Ibrahim said, "Come, let's go to his house this afternoon, see who he is and what he has to say." I thought a little bit and then agreed.

After work, we went to the man's house on my motorcycle in the afternoon. His house was a little after Sayyid Khandan Bridge. We looked for his house in the sideroads and as we were approaching his house, he was also just getting home. I recognised him from the photo that was glued to the report. He was sitting in his Mercedes-Benz, waiting for his garage door to open. A woman with no hijab on got out of the car, opened the door and then he drove the car in. I exclaimed, "What did I tell you, Ibrahim? I told you his wife doesn't wear hijab!" He replied, "First let's speak with him and then make a judgement." I parked the motorcycle in front of his house and Ibrahim went and rang the bell. The man, who was still in his courtyard, came to the door. He was a man with a large physique and a clean-shaven face. He was surprised to see me and Ibrahim in that neighbourhood as our faces were different from those in the neighbourhood [as they mostly didn't have beards]. He looked at us and asked, "Can I help you?"

I thought to myself that if I was in Ibrahim's place right now, I would be terrified, but Ibrahim said salaam calmly and with a smile and said, "My name is Ibrahim Hadi and I have a few questions I need to ask you which is why I have come today." The man replied, "Your name is very familiar. I think I heard it a few days ago at work. You work in the department inspection office, am I right?" Ibrahim laughed and said yes. The man became very flustered and insisted that we come inside but Ibrahim said, "Thank you, but we just want to speak to you for a few minutes and then we will be on our way."

Ibrahim started speaking with him. He spoke for about an hour, but it didn't feel that long. Ibrahim spoke to him about everything and gave him an example about each subject about why those things he was doing were improper. He said, "Look, my friend, your wife is for yourself. She is not to be on show for others. Do you know how many youths will fall into sin by seeing your wife without a hijab? Similarly, during work, you should not be using swear words or making inappropriate jokes with your employees, especially women as the head of the federation. You were the champion of your field previously, but a real champion is one who prevents himself from falling into error." Then he started speaking of the Revolution, the martyrs, the Imam (ra) and the enemies of the country. The man agreed with Ibrahim completely. In conclusion, Ibrahim said, "Look, my dear friend, this is the order to dismiss you from your job." The man was shocked and looked at us, frightened. Ibrahim grinned, tore the letter and said, "Think about what I said, my dear friend!" We then bade farewell, got on the motorcycle and left. As we were leaving the street, I looked back. I could still see the man looking at us.

I said, "Your words were very beautiful today, Ibrahim! They even influenced me." He laughed and said, "I didn't do anything! Only Allah, Allah put these words into my mind. Insha'Allah they affect him." He added, "I'm telling you; nothing influences people like proper conduct. Have you not read in the Qur'an where Allah says to the Prophet (s), 'If you were rough, harsh-hearted, people would have disbanded from you?" So, let's learn a bit from the Prophet (s)'s behaviour at least."

One or two months later, a new report arrived from that same federation; the head of the federation had changed significantly and so had his behaviour in the workplace. His wife would even come to the workplace in full hijab. I found Ibrahim and gave him the report. I was waiting for a reaction from him, but all he did was read it, thank God and then he changed the subject. I had no doubt that Ibrahim's sincerity had left an effect on the head of the federation and changed him this much.

TENDING TO PEOPLE

Narrator: Some of the martyr's friends

It is narrated from Imam Sadiq (a) that Allah said, "The servants are like my family. The most beloved to Me are those who are the kindest to the other servants and the most persistent in addressing their needs."[47]

There was a large gathering on Shaheed Sa'eedi Street. Ibrahim and I went closer and asked what was going on. Someone told us, "This child is mentally ill. He here every day. He takes dirty water out of the gutter with a bucket and throws it at well-dressed people." The crowd started to disperse slowly. A man wearing a very nice suit who was drenched by the boy complained, "I don't know what to do with this retarded child!" That man left, and we were alone with that child.

Ibrahim asked the child, "Why do you throw water at people?" The child giggled and said, "It makes me happy!" Ibrahim

---

47   Al-Kafi, vol. 2, p. 199

thought a little and asked, "Does anyone tell you to throw water?" The child replied, "They give me five riyals and tell me who to throw water at." He then pointed across the road where three hooligans were laughing. Ibrahim started walking towards them but stopped, turned to the child, and asked the boy where his house was. The child gave him his address and Ibrahim said, "If you stop annoying people, I will give you ten riyals a day, okay?" The boy agreed and when we reached his home, Ibrahim spoke to his mother and in this manner, Ibrahim removed an obstacle from the path of the people.

We were working as department inspectors at the Sports Department. One day after receiving our salary and finishing work, Ibrahim asked me if I had brought my motorcycle and I told him I had. He said, "If you are not doing anything right now, let's go to the shop." Ibrahim spent nearly his entire salary on rice, meat, soap and other things as if somebody had given him a shopping list.

We then headed towards the Majidiyyeh Neighbourhood and he knocked on a door. An old lady who didn't seem to be wearing proper hijab opened the door. Ibrahim gave her everything he bought. I noticed that she was wearing a cross around her neck. I was very surprised and on the way back home, I asked Ibrahim if she was an Armenian Christian. "Yes, why?" Ibrahim replied. I stopped on the side of the road, turned the bike off and said to Ibrahim furiously, "There are so many poor Muslim families out there, but you went to help the Christians?!" Ibrahim replied while sitting behind me, "There is someone to help the Muslims. Also, a charity has been set up. However, these poor people [Christians] have no one to help them. By doing these things, their problems are resolved on one hand and on the other, they start to love Imam

Khomeini and the Revolution."

---

26 years after Ibrahim's martyrdom, we had collected all the memories from his life and the book was ready to be printed. As I was in the mosque, one of the people of the congregation called me and said, "If you need any help with organising Ibrahim's memorial ceremony, I am at your service." I asked him, surprised, "Did you know Shaheed Hadi? Had you seen him?" He replied, "No, I didn't anything about Shaheed Hadi until I attended his memorial ceremony last year, but I am heavily indebted to him." I was in a rush to leave but I was intrigued, so I came closer and asked him, "How are you indebted to him?"

The man replied, "In last year's commemoratory session, they distributed keyrings with Shaheed Hadi's face on it. I took one and put it on my car keys. A few days ago, I was returning from a journey with my family and on the way back, we stopped at a motel. When we wanted to get back in the car, I realised that I'd left my keys in the car and the doors were locked. I asked my wife if she had the spare keys, but she said, "My keys are in my bag which is in the car." I was worried. I tried everything but the door wouldn't open. It was unpleasantly cold. I thought of breaking the window, but the journey home was long, and it was very cold outside. Suddenly, I saw Shaheed Hadi's keyring. It was as if he was looking at me from the keyring. I looked at him and said, "Agha Ibrahim, I heard that as long as you were alive you would help people, and a martyr is always alive." I then prayed to Allah, "Oh Allah, by the right of Shaheed Ibrahim's reputation, solve my problem!"

At that moment, I put my hand into my pocket, and I took my home keys out. I unconsciously put one of the keys inside the car and turned it. To everyone's surprise, the door opened! We all got into the car, overjoyed. I then looked at Shaheed Hadi and said,

"Thank you. Insha'Allah I'll be able to repay you." My wife asked which key I opened the car door with before we left and I told her, "You're right, which key was it?" I got out and tried each of my keys one by one. I tried them a few times but none of the keys would even fit in the lock! As I was standing there, I sighed and said, "Thank you, Agha Ibrahim; even after your martyrdom, you resolve people's problems!"

KURDISTAN

Narrator: Mahdi Faridvand

It was the summer of 1979 and we were standing outside Salman Mosque after Dhuhr and Asr prayers. As I was talking with Ibrahim, one of our friends ran up to us and said, "Did you hear what Imam Khomeini's message?!" We asked, "No, what happened?!" He told us, "The Imam has ordered us to help the soldiers in Kurdistan break the siege they are under." Mohammad Shahroudi came along and told us, "Qasem Tashakkori, Naser Kermani and I are going to Kurdistan." Ibrahim said, "I'm also coming," and then we left to get ready for the journey.

By four o'clock in the afternoon, eleven of us jumped into a truck set for Kurdistan. We had one G3 rifle, four crates of guns and a few grenades as our ammunition. Many of the roads were blocked and we were occasionally forced to travel through the desert. With the help of Allah, we managed to reach Sanandaj by the afternoon the next day.

We entered the city, completely unaware of our whereabouts. We stopped in front of a newspaper stand and Ibrahim got out to ask where the army barracks were. Suddenly, I heard him shout, "Why are you selling these things, you corrupt man?!" I looked outside, and I saw that there were a few cases of alcoholic beverages besides the stall. Ibrahim immediately took his gun and started shooting the bottles. The bottles broke and the alcohol spilt everywhere. He then broke the rest and headed towards the shopkeeper in anger. The young seller was terrified, and he hid in the corner of the stall. Ibrahim looked at him and said calmly, "Are you not a Muslim, my son? What are these impurities that you are selling? Has Allah not said in the Qur'an, 'these impurities are from Satan so stay away from them'[48]?" The youth kept nodding his head in agreement. He was constantly saying, "I know I did wrong. Please forgive me!" Ibrahim spoke with the young man for a little while and then they came out of the stall together. The youth then showed us the way towards the army barracks.

We set off towards the army barracks, the sound of G3 rifles being fired breaking the silence which had descended upon the city. Everyone on the road was staring at us as we were moving around the city without knowing where we were. We eventually arrived at the Sanandaj Army Barracks. The walls of the barracks were covered with sandbags, making the place look more like a fort; there was no sign of the actual building! They refused to open the door regardless of how much we knocked and rather, they told us from behind the door, "The city belongs to the anti-revolutionaries. Don't stay here. Go to the airport!" We told them, "We've come here to help you. At least tell us where the airport is!" One of the soldiers came to the wall and said, "This place is not safe, they might even come and hit you with a car. Leave the city from that way now. If you go down that road, you will eventually reach the airport. The revolutionary forces are stationed there."

We left for the airport and only there did we find out what was happening in Sanandaj. Apart from the army barracks and the airport, the whole city belonged to the anti-revolutionaries. Three army battalions, as well as one battalion of the IRGC,[49] were stationed in the airport. Mortar shells were constantly being fired

---

48   Referring to Surah Ma'idah, verse 90

49   The Iranian Revolutionary Guard Corps

from inside the city towards the airport. It was there that we met Mohammad Boroujerdi for the first time, a youth with a golden beard and hair and a handsome and smiling face. Despite the poor conditions, Brother Boroujerdi was still able to manage his troops well and later, we found out that he was the commander of the army in the west of Iran.

The next day, we had a meeting with Brother Boroujerdi as well as the commanders of the army. He said, "I believe many forces are coming to Kurdistan because of the Imam's order and the anti-revolutionaries are terrified. They have two main strongholds in the city. We must plan to attack them." Everybody gave their opinions, and Ibrahim said, "As far as I understand, the residents of the city have no connection with them. It is better to attack one of the anti-revolutionary strongholds and then if we are successful, we attack the next one." Everybody agreed with this strategy and we were told to prepare the soldiers for battle, but they decided to send the IRGC forces to Paveh that day and we were left with the army soldiers.

Ibrahim and some of our other friends visited each of the trenches and talked with the soldiers. They spoke to them and tried to raise their morale. They then bought a whole truck full of watermelons and gave them out to the soldiers. They would employ these kinds of methods to try and make friends with the soldiers and they would prepare them in different manners.

One morning, Agha Khalkhali joined our troops and in the meantime, a few other soldiers arrived at Sanandaj Airport. After getting ready, the ammunition was distributed among the soldiers. We attacked one of the strongholds before noon. We besieged the stronghold faster than we had expected. Eventually, they surrendered, and we arrested most of them. Inside the stronghold, not only did we find a lot of ammunition, but we also found lots of American dollars and fake passports and ID cards. Ibrahim put all of them in a sack and sent them to the army commander.

The second stronghold was captured without any fighting like the first and once again, the city had fallen to the hands of the revolutionaries. I will not forget what the commander said that day, "Even if we had waited a few years, my soldiers would never have had the courage to plan such an attack. We are indebted to Agha Ibrahim and his friends who managed to lift their morale by making friends with them."

During that period, the commanders taught Ibrahim and the other soldiers the art and strategies of war. These classes transformed mere foot soldiers into experienced warriors, and the fruits were reaped in the era of the Holy Defence.

The war in Sanandaj didn't last long even though there were still some scuffles in the other Kurdish cities. We returned to Tehran in August 1979, but Qasem and a few of our other friends remained in Kurdistan and joined Shaheed Chamran's[50] troops. Once he returned to Tehran, Ibrahim resigned from his job at the Sports Department and started teaching. Of course, they didn't want him to move from the department, but after insisting, they accepted his resignation. He then started a career in which we needed and still need many people like Ibrahim.

THE EXEMPLARY TEACHER

Narrator: Abbas Hadi

Ibrahim would say, "If we want the Revolution to remain steadfast and for the next generation to become revolutionary, we need to work in schools because the people who didn't experience the conditions during the time of the oppressor will take control of the future of our country." He would be disappointed when he would see non-revolutionary people teach in schools and he would say, "The best revolutionary forces must teach in the schools, especially

---

50 Iran's minister of defence from 1979-80. He was martyred in 1981.

high schools." For this reason, he left an easy job for a more difficult one with a lower salary. However, he never thought about worldly belongings. He used to say, "Allah provides sustenance. The blessing of money is important, but things that are done in the way of Allah have much more blessing." He started working in two schools. He worked as a sports teacher at Abu Reyhan High School in Province 14 and an Arabic teacher at a Montessori school for deprived children in Province 15.

He didn't teach Arabic for very long as he left midyear without mentioning a reason. One day, the principal of the school came to me and we spoke. He said, "I'm begging you; you are Agha Hadi's brother. Please talk to him and ask him to come back to school." I asked him what had happened and he told me, "The truth is, in the first hour every morning, Agha Ibrahim would give his own money to one of the students to buy bread and cheese for the class. He believed that as most of the people in this area were deprived, this meant that most of the children were coming into school hungry and hungry children don't understand the lesson. I reproached Ibrahim and said, 'You have disorganised the order of this school. There was never a problem like this before you came.' I then shouted at him, 'You don't have the right to do these things here anymore!' Agha Hadi resigned from this school and now works full-time elsewhere. Now all the children and employees want me to bring him back. Everyone praises his good conduct and teaching methods. In the short time he taught here, he managed to buy stationery items and school necessities for the poor and orphan children without my knowledge." I spoke with Ibrahim about what the principal had told me but there was nothing I could do; he had already started working elsewhere.

As well as teaching sports at Abu Reyhan High School, Ibrahim would also incorporate good conduct and akhlaq into his lessons. The students were impressed by him and loved him as they had heard of all his achievements. He would make sure to always wear a nice suit to school in a time when most of the revolutionary youth wouldn't care about their appearance. His handsome and bright face coupled with his captivating words and proper conduct made him the complete teacher. He was very skilled in keeping the class in order; he laughed when he needed to and was strict when needed. At break time, he would come to the playground and most of the students would gather around him. He was the first to come into school and the last to leave, and there were always students surrounding him.

At a time where political discussions were widespread, Ibrahim chose the one place where he was able to serve the Revolution the most. I remember that a few of his students were being influenced by certain political movements so one night, Ibrahim invited them to the mosque and he also invited a few revolutionary people who were active in political discussions so that they could have a question and answer session. That night, all the students' questions were answered, and the session ended at two o'clock in the morning!

In the 1979-80 academic year, Ibrahim was named the most exemplary teacher in Tehran even though it was his first and last year of teaching. At the end of September 1980, Ibrahim's services were requested in Province 12 of Tehran, but he was no longer able to teach anymore due to the start of the war. That year, Ibrahim had many occupations including teaching at school, working with the revolutionary committee, exercise, going to the mosque, reciting for Imam Husayn (a), attending many revolutionary programmes and so on, which was the work of more than just one person!

THE HEAD OF SPORT
Narrator: Memoirs of Shaheed Reza Houryar

It was April 1980 and I was working as head of sport at Shuhada High School. Abu Reyhan High School was next to our school where Ibrahim worked as a sports teacher. I went to visit him, and we spoke for a bit. I was impressed by his behaviour and principles. He asked me after class, "Do you want to play one-on-one volleyball?" I started laughing because I had gone to the global championships with the national team and I considered myself as one of the best. Now this nobody wanted to play against me one-on-one! I agreed but I thought to myself, "I will play badly so he doesn't feel embarrassed."

He hit the first serve so hard, I couldn't reach it. He then hit the second, the third and so on. I went pale from embarrassment because all the students were watching. He would serve so strangely; it was very difficult to return the serve. He glanced at me and then served the ball very lightly. I got my first point of the match, and then my second, my third and so on. He didn't want me to feel embarrassed so he would purposefully hit the balls out of bound. I tied Ibrahim's score and my reputation was preserved! I threw the ball to him for him to serve in the second half and he caught it. As he was about to serve, we heard the adhan. He put the ball on the ground, stood towards the *Qibla*[51] and started reciting the adhan. The children left, some to do *wudu*[52] and some to go home. He started praying right there in the playground and the children prayed behind him. A big congregation gathered behind Ibrahim. When he finished praying, he looked back at me, shook my hand and said, "Agha Reza, a rivalry is beautiful when there is friendship involved."[53]

---

51   The direction of Makkah towards which Muslims pray
52   Ritual ablutions performed before praying
53   Commander Reza Houryar went to the global championships with the deaf volleyball team and his team won (even though he wasn't deaf). He was martyred in Operation Karbala 5.

PRAYING ON TIME

Narrator: Some of the martyr's friends

All his activities revolved around prayers. He would pray on time in even the most difficult circumstances, and he would mainly pray in the mosque and in congregation. He would also invite others to pray in congregation. He was living proof of the saying of Imam Ali (a), "Whoever regularly attends the mosque will benefit from one of eight: a brother who will make friends with him in the way of Allah, new knowledge, mercy that was lying in wait for him, advice which will save him from destruction, words which will guide him or he will abstain from sinning."[54] Even before the Revolution, he would pray Fajr in the mosque in congregation.

His attitude towards prayer reminds me of Shaheed Rajaei's[55] words, "Don't say to prayers that you are busy, rather, tell your work that it is time for prayer."

The best example of this was the congregational prayers in the ring of the gym. When it was prayer time and the youth were busy exercising, Ibrahim would stop the exercise and start congregational prayers. Many times, whilst travelling or while we were on the warfront, he would start reciting the adhan when it would become prayer time and he would encourage everyone to leave the vehicle and pray in congregation. Ibrahim's loud call of the adhan would encourage everyone to come and pray with him. He was the embodiment of these beautiful words of Prophet Muhammad (s), "Allah has promised that the one who recites the

---

54   Mawa'idh al-Adadiyyah, p. 281
55   The president of Iran from 2nd of August to the 30th of August 1981 when he was martyred in parliament by a hidden bomb

adhan, the one who does wudu and the one who takes part in congregational prayers in the mosque will enter heaven without judgement."[56]

At that time, Ibrahim had made friends with the youth who would attend the mosques of his neighbourhood. During his youth, he bought himself an *'aba*[57] and would pray with the cloak on most of the time.

One night in 1980, the revolutionary committee meeting continued until midnight. There were two hours left until Fajr. Ibrahim gathered the youth and started to narrate his memories of Kurdistan which were both interesting and funny. He kept the youth awake until Fajr, prayed in congregation and then sent them home.

Ibrahim told the leader of the committee, "If these youth went home at that hour, we don't know if they would have woken up for Fajr or not. You should either end the meeting early or keep them here until Fajr so that they don't miss their prayers."

Although Ibrahim was a light-hearted person during the day, he would wake up before dawn to pray Salat ul-Layl[58] and he would try to keep this a secret from others. The closer he came to

---

56   Mustadrak al-Wasa'il, vol. 6, pg. 448

57   An *'aba* is the Arabic word for a cloak, and it is *mustahabb* to wear this over one's shoulders while praying

58   Salat ul-Layl is a 11-unit prayer which is prayed from between midnight and Fajr. Imam Sadiq (a) said, "Every single good deed that the servant carries out has a reward mentioned for it in the Qur'an except for Salat ul-Layl, for verily Allah has not expressed its reward because of the great significance it holds with Him. Thus, He says, *"Their sides vacate their beds to supplicate their Lord in fear and hope... No one knows what has been kept hidden for them of comfort as a reward for what they used to do."* (Bihar al-Anwar, vol. 8, p. 126)

his martyrdom, the longer he would stay awake at night. He knew well that one of the signs of a true Shia is that they stay up during dawn and pray Salat ul-Layl.

He would regularly recite Dua Kumayl[59] and Dua Nudbah[60]. He would recite the *duas* and *ziyarahs*[61] for each day after Fajr. He would recite Ziyarah Ashura[62] daily and if he wasn't able to, he would make sure to recite the final salaam of it. He was always whispering the ninth verse of Surah Yasin. One time, I said to him, "Agha Ibrahim, this verse is to protect you from enemies but there are no enemies here!" He looked at me meaningfully and asked, "Is there any enemy greater than Satan?"

One day, we were talking about teenagers and the importance of prayers. Ibrahim recalled, "When my father passed away, I was extremely upset. After the guests left on the first night, I went to sleep without praying as if to show my anger towards Allah. As soon as I fell asleep, I saw my father in a dream. He opened the *door* to our house and walked straight to my room furiously. He stood in front of me and stared at me. At that moment, I jumped from my sleep. My father's look at me was very meaningful. There was still time left to pray so I got up, did wudu and prayed."

Ibrahim gave a lot of importance to the Friday prayers. Whenever he was in Tehran, he would participate in Friday prayers

---

[59] Dua Kumayl is a supplication narrated from Imam Ali (a) by his companion, Kumayl ibn Ziyad. It is recommended to recite this supplication on Friday eves.

[60] Dua Nudbah is a supplication recommended to be recited on the morning of the four Eids which include Eid al-Fitr, Eid al-Adha, Eid al-Ghadir and Friday.

[61] *Ziyarah* has two definitions: a) a series of salutations upon an Infallible or a companion of an Infallible and b) visiting the grave of an Infallible or one of the companions of the Infallibles. In this context, we are mentioning the former definition.

[62] Ziyarah Ashura is a series of salutations narrated from Imam Baqir (a) in which one sends salutations upon Imam Husayn (a), his family and his companions. It is recommended to recite this *ziyarah* on the Day of Ashura or to be read for forty consecutive nights if one needs something.

even though he was mostly in Kurdistan or on the warfront. He would say, "You don't know how many blessings Friday prayers have." Imam Sadiq (a) said, "There is no foot that strives towards attending the Friday prayers except that Allah will prevent it from touching the Hellfire."[63]

AN ENCOUNTER WITH A THIEF

Narrator: Abbas Hadi

As we were sitting with our guests in the living room, we heard a loud commotion on the road. Ibrahim ran to the window to find out what was going on and he saw that somebody was trying to steal his brother-in-law's motorcycle. He ran to the door. One of our neighbours had kicked the motorcycle and the thief had fallen with it. A piece of iron that was lying on the ground had severed the thief's hand and blood was pouring from it. The thief's face was full of worry and fright. He was crying out in pain as Ibrahim arrived. Ibrahim picked the motorcycle up and told him, "Get on quickly!" They went to the hospital and got his hand bandaged.

After that, they went to the mosque. After prayers, Ibrahim sat beside him and asked, "Why do you steal? You're only earning haram money!" The thief was crying and said, "I know all of this. I'm jobless and I have a wife and kids to take care of. I come from a small village and my circumstances forced my hand!" Ibrahim thought a little and then he went to speak to one of the people at the mosque. He returned happily and said, "Thank God, I found a good job for you. From tomorrow, you can go to." He then gave him some money and told him, "Take this money and ask Allah to help

---

63 Namaz dar Ayeen-e Hadees, pg. 101, saying 215

you. Always try to earn halal money, as haram money will destroy your life. Even if halal money is little, it still has so much blessing!"

THE BEGINNING OF THE WAR
Narrator: Taqi Masgarha

On the morning of Monday, the 22nd of September 1980, I saw Ibrahim and his brother busy moving furniture about. I said salaam and said, "Qasem is going to Kurdistan this afternoon and we're going with him." He asked if something had happened and I told him, "There are reports that new fights may break out." He replied, "Ok, I will come with you if I can." Noon that day, the Iraqis started the war with an airstrike. Everybody in the streets was looking up at the sky. At four o'clock in the afternoon, Qasem Tashakkori came with Ali Khorramdel in a Deer jeep full of ammunition. I got in and as we were about to leave, Ibrahim also came and got in. I asked, "Were you not moving furniture?" He replied, "I moved the furniture to the new house and came."

We reached Sarpol-e Zahab before noon on the second day of the war after a strenuous journey through the desert. None of us could believe our eyes. People were fleeing from the city in droves. We could hear missiles and mortar shells exploding from inside the city. We didn't know what to do. We found a small way into the city and I saw one of the soldiers of the IRGC waving at us. I said, "Qasem! The soldiers are telling us to hurry up." Suddenly, Ibrahim called out, pointing, "Look over there!" The Iraqi tanks were advancing from behind the hill and constantly shooting. Some of the bullets hit the side of our car but all thanks to Allah, we were all safe.

Once we entered the city, one of the IRGC soldiers came up to us and asked, "Who are you? I kept telling you not to come but you sped up!" Qasem asked, "What is happening here? Who is the commander?" The soldier replied, "Agha Boroujerdi is in the city with the other soldiers. The Iraqis occupied most of the city this morning, but we forced them back with our attack." We set off further into the city and parked the car in a safe place. Qasem prayed two units of prayer right there. After he finished, Ibrahim went up to him and asked, "Qasem, what was that prayer?" He replied very calmly, "In Kurdistan, I always prayed to Allah so that I wouldn't be taken prisoner or wounded while fighting against the enemies of Islam and the Revolution. However, I prayed to Allah for martyrdom this time. I can't endure this world anymore." Ibrahim listened to Qasim's words carefully.

We then went to meet Mohammad Boroujerdi who knew Qasem from before and was excited to see him. After a little conversation, he pointed in a certain direction and said, "Two battalions have gone that way and they don't have a commander. My dear Qasem, go and see if you can bring them back into the city." We all went together. The place was full of armed soldiers ready to serve but they were shocked. They weren't expecting such an attack from Iraq. Qasem and Ibrahim went forward and started speaking with them. They spoke in such a moving manner that the soldiers started to feel the honour and chivalry in their words. In conclusion, they said, "Whoever is a man with honour and does not want the Ba'athists[64] to touch their people, come with us!" Their words led to nearly all the soldiers joining the advance. Qasem arranged the forces and we came back inside the city. As we were barricading the city, some of the soldiers informed us they had mortar shells. Qasem found a good place to station them and they started shooting. After firing a few mortar shells, the Iraqi tanks retreated behind their lines. This helped to increase the morale of the soldiers.

As the sun was setting, Qasem chose a house that was close

---

64   The party which was headed by Saddam Hussein from 1968-2003, the party was the one which attacked Iran

to the trenches where the soldiers were stationed as our base. He asked me to call Ibrahim to read Dua Tawassul as it was Tuesday night. As I left the house, Qasem started praying Maghrib. As I was walking away, suddenly, a missile exploded outside the door of the house. I thought to myself, "Thank God Qasem went into the room," but I still ran back. Ibrahim came running when he heard the explosion. We couldn't believe our eyes when we entered the room; a piece of debris the size of a lentil grain had broken through the window and struck Qasem in his chest. Qasem got what he wished for in the middle of his prayers! Mohammad Boroujerdi was deeply hurt when he heard the news. That night, we recited Dua Tawassul beside Qasem's body and we sent his body back to Tehran the next day.

The day after, we went to the main headquarters. They put us in charge of the arsenal and handed over a school which was full of ammunition. We stayed there for a day before moving it all outside of the city because it was dangerous. Ibrahim used to repeatedly say jokingly, "Guys, remember Allah a lot in this place because if a mortar shell were to land here, there will be nothing of us left!" Once we evacuated the ammunition depot, we returned to the warfront. Trenches had been dug to the west of Sarpol-e Zahab. Some of the trained commanders including Asghar Vesali and Ali Qorbani had been sent to lead the soldiers there. These commanders had founded a guerrilla battalion in Paveh named 'The Red Bandanas' and they had now come with their soldiers to Sarpol-e Zahab.

We went to look around the city and we found a few familiar faces including Mohammad Shahroudi, Majid Faridvand and some others. We all headed to the front line of resistance against the Iraqis together. The commander told us in the trenches at the top of the hill, "This hill opposite of us is where we are currently fighting the Iraqis. From the next hill onwards, it is Iraqi territory." A few minutes later, we saw an Iraqi soldier moving and the soldiers started shooting. Ibrahim shouted, "What are you doing?! You're going to finish all of your bullets!" Everybody went quiet. Ibrahim, who had learnt the art of war during the courses in Kurdistan, said, "Wait until the enemy comes closer and then shoot." In the meantime, the Iraqis started shooting from the bottom of the hill. Missiles and mortars were constantly raining down upon us. They then started advancing towards our trenches. The soldiers who had just held a gun for the first time started to retreat to the trenches behind us. We were all frightened. The commander shouted, "Wait! Don't be afraid!" Moments later, the sounds of the Iraqis' gunshots became less so I peeked outside the trench. The Iraqis had come extremely close to our trenches. Ibrahim and a few soldiers then mounted an attack on the Iraqis. They jumped out of the trenches yelling 'Allahu Akbar!' and in a matter of minutes, many Iraqi soldiers had been killed and wounded. Ibrahim and the others took eleven Iraqis prisoner and the rest fled. Ibrahim paraded them around the city and many of the soldiers regained morale by seeing them. A few people were taking photos of the prisoners and some even took pictures with Ibrahim himself as a keepsake!

An hour later, we returned to Sarpol-e Zahab. They informed us that as the roads being closed, Qasem's body was still in the garrison. We went there and on the fifth day of the war, we returned Qasem's body to Tehran in his car. A glorious funeral was held in Tehran and the first martyr of the Holy Defence from our neighbourhood was laid to rest. Many people came and Ali Khorramdel was shouting, "O' my martyred commander, your path will continue!"

THE SECOND APPEARANCE

Narrator: Amir Monjar

On the 30th of September 1980, we accompanied the military strategists to the war provinces. On the way, we stopped for a bit at the army headquarters in Hamadan. It was time for the adhan of Dhuhr. Over there, we met Agha Boroujerdi who was also on his way to the war provinces with a few of the IRGC soldiers. Ibrahim was busy reciting the adhan and everyone was getting ready to pray. It was a very spiritual atmosphere. Mohammad Boroujerdi asked me, "Agha Amir, where is Ibrahim from?" I replied, "He is from our neighbourhood near 17 Shahrivar Street and Khorasan Square." Agha Boroujerdi said, "He has a beautiful voice. I saw him once or twice in the war provinces. He's a daring and courageous youth. If you can, bring him to me in Kermanshah." After the adhan, we prayed in congregation and we set off.

This was the second time we had come to Sarpol-e Zahab. Asghar Vesali had arranged his troops and after that, the area was relatively organised. Asghar was a brave and valiant commander, and Ibrahim loved him very much. Ibrahim used to always say, "I have never seen a guerrilla soldier with such courage and organisational skills. He has even brought his wife to the warfront. He visits all of the war provinces in his car which resembles an arsenal." Asghar also felt the same way towards Ibrahim. Once, when he wanted to carry out a reconnaissance operation, he took Ibrahim with him. When they returned, Asghar said, "I fought in Lebanon before the Revolution. I was in Kurdistan for the entire '79 war, but this youth [Ibrahim] is both very strong and understands warfare well although he hasn't had any formal military training." For this reason, he would take Ibrahim's advice when planning operations. In one attack, they managed to destroy eight tanks and take a few enemy soldiers captive without giving any casualties.

Asghar Vesali converted one of the buildings of the Abu Dhar Garrison into a shelter for the volunteer troops. He established a form of order in the city by making them register, gathering their information and dividing them into battalions.

Once the city became calmer, Ibrahim started *Varzesh-e Bastani* with a few of his friends again. As he didn't have a drum to make a beat for the people exercising, Ibrahim used a pot and would recite with his beautiful voice every morning. Asghar would be at the centre of the exercise, holding a G3 rifle as his weights. They used mortar shells, rifles and other weaponry as weights. One of the commanders said, "Many people had stayed in the city at that time, so soldiers and nurses would come together in the mornings to do *Varzesh-e Bastani*." Ibrahim would recite with a loud voice and Asghar would exercise in the centre. They managed to make the city seem lively and make the others hopeful too. Truly, Ibrahim was an outstanding person!

Imam Sadiq (a) said, "Every single good deed that the servant carries out has a reward mentioned for it in the Qur'an except for Salat ul-Layl, for verily Allah has not expressed its reward because of the great significance it holds with Him. Thus, He says, "Their sides vacate their beds to supplicate their Lord in fear and hope... No one knows what has been kept hidden for them of comfort as a reward for what they used to do.""[65]

During our short stay in Sarpol-e Zahab, Ibrahim would normally wake up two hours before the adhan of Fajr and walk away. He would say that he was going to check on the others, but I had no doubt that he was praying Salat ul-Layl. Once, I saw Ibrahim wake up an hour before the adhan of Fajr and he used a tub of water to do ghusl[66] and prayed Salat ul-Layl.

---

65   Mizan al-Hikmah, saying no. 3665

66   Major ritual ablution where one washes their head and neck then the right side of their body and then the left side of their body.

THE TASBIH OF LADY FATIMAH (A)
Narrator: Amir Sepehr-Nejad

It was the 4th of October 1980, and it had been two days since Ibrahim went missing. I went to the committee in charge of the prisoners of war, but they hadn't heard anything either. I was awake until midnight and devastated as I didn't know where my best friend was. After Fajr prayers the next morning, I went out into the courtyard. That morning, the Abu Dhar Garrison was relatively quiet. I sat on the floor in the courtyard and thought about all the memories I shared with Ibrahim. The day had not fully broken yet when the door of the base opened, and a few people came in. I looked towards the door and I tried to make out their faces. Suddenly, I jumped up; It was him! It was Ibrahim! I ran up to him and hugged him. My joy at that moment was indescribable.

An hour later, we were sitting with the rest of the soldiers and Ibrahim told us what had happened in those three days he was missing:

We advanced in an APC[67]. We didn't know how far the Iraqis had advanced. We were surrounded next to a hill. Around one hundred Iraqis were shooting at us from both on top of the hill and from the valley. Us five took cover in a ditch and we started firing back. We resisted until sunset and when it became completely dark, the Iraqi soldiers fell back. The two people who knew the area were both martyred. We left the ditch and there was nobody around. We then went behind the hill and into the trees where we hid the martyrs' bodies. We were hungry and tired. We guessed the direction of the Qibla from the direction in which the sun set. After praying, I said to my friends, "Let's recite the *tasbih*[68] of Lady Fatimah (a) to resolve the problems we are in." I added, "The Prophet (s) taught his daughter this tasbih when her daily life was

---

67 Armoured personnel carrier

68 Praise which consists of reading Allahu Akbar (God is greater than any description) 34 times, Alhamdulillah (All praise is due to God) 33 times and Subhan Allah (Glory be to God) 33 times

riddled with problems." After reciting the tasbih, we returned to our previous coverage.

There were no Iraqis in sight, and we were running low on provisions. Suddenly, I noticed that there were a few bodies of Iraqi soldiers lying beside the hill. We took their weapons, ammo and grenades as well as some food. We got ready to leave, but we didn't know which direction to go. It was dark and we were in a desert. I had a rosary in my hands, and I was constantly doing dhikr[69]. Even though we were in the middle of enemy territory, tired and in the dark, I still felt strangely calm.

Around midnight, we found a road in the middle of the desert which we followed to a military base. It had a radar station protected by a few guards. We could also see garrisons inside the base as well. We didn't know where we were and we didn't have any hope of surviving, so I made a drastic decision. I did an istikharah[70] with my rosary and it came out good, so we began. We started throwing grenades and shooting at the base so that we could destroy it. Once we destroyed the radar, all three of us left and an hour later, we started walking again.

In the morning, we found a safe place and we rested for the whole day. I couldn't believe how calm I was. As night fell, we started moving again and we managed to reach you with Allah's help.

He added, "What we had seen on this journey had all been a gift from Allah. The tasbih of Lady Fatimah (a) helped us with many of our problems. The enemy fears our troops due to their lack of faith. We should do guerilla attacks as much as we can to prevent their attacks."

---

69   Praise of Allah

70   Asking Allah for help or guidance

SHAHRAK AL-MAHDI

Narrators: Ali Moqaddam, Hosein Jahanbakhsh

One month passed since the beginning of the war and Ibrahim had gone to Shahrak al-Mahdi on the outskirts of Sarpol-e Zahab along with Haj Hosein and a few other friends to set up defensive trenches against the enemy there. After praying Fajr in congregation, I noticed that the soldiers were searching for Ibrahim. I asked what had happened and they told me, "Nobody has seen Ibrahim since midnight." I started to look for him with the others in the trenches and from the watchtowers. An hour later, one of the guards shouted, "A few people are coming towards us from the groves in front of us!" The groves were exactly where the enemy was positioned. I immediately went to the watchtower to see what the others were looking at. We saw thirteen Iraqis coming towards us, their hands bound. Ibrahim and another soldier were walking behind them carrying many guns, grenades and ammo clips. No one could believe that Ibrahim could do such a thing with just one other soldier, especially at a time where there was a shortage of weapons and ammunition in Shahrak al-Mahdi to an extent that some of the soldiers didn't even have a gun.

One of the excited soldiers slapped the first Iraqi prisoner strongly and shouted, "Cursed Iraqi!" Everyone went quiet for a moment. Ibrahim walked past all the prisoners and went up to the youth. He put down the guns he was carrying on his shoulder one by one and then yelled, "Why did you slap him in the face?!" The soldier was taken aback and replied, "What did I do wrong? He's the enemy." Ibrahim stared at him and said, "Firstly, he was an enemy but now he is our prisoner. Secondly, these people don't know why they are fighting with us. Now tell me, should we behave like this?!" The soldier replied, "I'm sorry, I became a little bit excited." He turned around, kissed the prisoner on his forehead and asked for forgiveness. The Iraqi prisoner was looking at all of us with surprise and then he turned to Ibrahim. His wonderous gaze at Ibrahim spoke many words!

Two months into the war, Ibrahim came to Tehran on leave and I went to see him with a few friends. Ibrahim told us some memories he had from the war, but he wouldn't talk about himself. We started speaking about the prayers and the worship of the soldiers. Ibrahim smiled and said:

"At the beginning of our time in the Al-Mahdi Province, five youth joined our battalion. They had come from a village to fight on the frontline together. I realised after a few days that they didn't pray, so I spoke to them one day and I realised that they were very simple people. They were illiterate and they didn't know how to pray. They had come to the warfront because of their love for Imam Khomeini. They also wanted to learn how to pray. I first taught them how to do wudu, and then I called over one of the soldiers and said, "He's your leader in prayer. Do whatever he does. I will be standing here reading the things to say so that you can slowly learn."

At that moment, Ibrahim couldn't stop laughing. A few minutes later, he continued:

"In the first unit of prayer while they were reciting Surah Fatihah, the Imam started scratching his head and all five of them started scratching their heads! I wanted to laugh, but I controlled myself. However, as the imam got up from sajdah[71], the turbah[72] got stuck to the Imam's head and he had to lean to his left to take it off. I then saw all the youth had leant to their left and stretched their arms out to imitate the imam! At that moment, I couldn't control myself and I started laughing."

---

71   Arabic for 'prostration'

72   A clay tablet on which Shias prostrate

THE PROBLEM SOLVER

Narrator: One of the martyr's friends

Someone asked the Prophet (s), "Which [kind of] believer has the most perfect faith?" to which he (s) replied, "The one who wages jihad with his life and wealth in the way of Allah."[73]

Commander Mohammad Kowsari (the former commander of the Hazrat-e Rasool (s) Division) said as he was narrating his memories, "At the beginning of the war in Sarpol-e Zahab, I told Ibrahim, "Brother Hadi, your salary is ready. Come to me and take it whenever you want." He asked me quietly when I was going to Tehran and I told him that I was due to leave at the end of the week. He said, "I will give you three addresses. When you go to Tehran, distribute my salary among these three households." I did as he said, and later, I found out that those three families were destitute."

I was on my way back from the warfront and by the time I reached Khorasan Square, I had no money left. I was on my way home and I started to think, "When I get home, my wife and my children will ask me for money." Also, what was I going to do about the rent?! Who could I turn to? Who could I ask for help? I thought about going to my brother's house, but his financial condition wasn't any better.

I was standing at the intersection and thought to myself, "Only Allah can help me. I can't think of anything else." As I was thinking, I saw Ibrahim coming towards me on his motorcycle. I was so happy to see him. As soon as he saw me, he got off his motorcycle and hugged me. We spoke for a few minutes and as he was about to leave, he asked, "Did you get your salary?" I replied,

---

73 Hukm al-Dhahirah, vol. 2, pg. 280

"No, I didn't get it but don't worry, it's not important." He put his hand in his pocket and took out some cash. I said, "I'm not going to take it. You need it yourself!" He said, "Take it as a loan. Whenever you get your salary, just pay it back to me." He put the money in my pocket, got back on his motorcycle and left.

That money had a lot of blessing in my life and it resolved many of my problems. For a while, I had no financial problems. I prayed for him a lot. That day, Allah sent Ibrahim to help me and as always, he resolved my problems.

THE SHAHEED ANDARZGU BATTALION

Narrator: Mostafa Saffar Harandi

A short while after the war started, the commanders of the army in the west of the country had a meeting and they decided that the volunteer troops and the soldiers of the IRGC should be dispatched to different parts of the country. Therefore, a group of soldiers from Sarpol-e Zahab were divided between Sumar, Mehran, Salehabad and Bostan. They appointed Hosein Allah-Karam, one of the warfront commanders, as the commander of the IRGC in Gilan-e Gharb and Naft Shahr. He went there with a few companies of soldiers from the 8th and 9th battalions of the IRGC. Ibrahim, who was good friends with Haj Hosein from his time in the gym, also went with him to Gilan-e Gharb and was appointed as the undersecretary of military operations.

Gilan-e Gharb is a city between several mountain ranges. It is 50 kilometres away from Naft Shahr and the Iraqi border and 70 kilometres south of Sarpol-e Zahab. Iraq had occupied most of the neighbouring areas and the surrounding mountains of the city.

At the beginning of the war, the 4th Army Corps of Iraq entered Gilan-e Gharb, but the resistance of the honourable men and women of this city forced them to retreat. During this attack, one of the women of this city killed two Iraqi soldiers with a sickle! After this, some of the residents left the city completely and some others would come during the day and would spend the night camped in tents on the highway to Islamabad.

The Zolfeqar Brigade of the Armed Forces was stationed in the town of Bansiran which is on the outskirts of Gilan-e Gharb. The IRGC was stationed in Gilan-e Gharb for a while and during this period, the only duty they had was to defend the city in the case of a possible attack from the enemy. Otherwise, no other action was expected of them.

A meeting was held, and the soldiers suggested that they should start doing ambush attacks in the same manner Dr Chamran and Asghar Vesali were doing in the South and Sarpol-e Zahab, respectively. They also suggested that a guerrilla battalion be established in Gilan-e Gharb. The commanders started to lay the foundation for such a battalion. Once everything was ready, they made Ibrahim and Javad Afrasyabi the operation directors of the battalion. The soldiers decided to name the battalion after Dr Beheshti (ra)[74], but Ayatollah Beheshti (ra) refused when he visited the area and suggested, "Because you are a guerrilla battalion, name your battalion after Shaheed Andarzgu, as he was the first to establish Islamic and guerrilla movements."

Ibrahim put three big photos of Imam Khomeini (ra), Ayatollah Beheshti (ra) and Ayatollah Khamenei on the wall in the battalion's base and from then on, the group started its activities.

---

74   Ayatollah Mohammad Hosseini Beheshti was a jurist and one of the leading figures of the Islamic Revolution and was also considered as the right-hand man of the late Imam (ra). He was martyred along with seventy-one others when a bomb hidden in a tape recorder by the Mujahedin-e Khalq Organisation (MKO) exploded during his address to parliament on the 28th of June 1981. His blessed body was laid to rest in Behesht-e Zahra.

The soldiers of this unorganised warfare battalion were truly unorganised. All kinds of people were in this battalion. From teenagers to old men, illiterates to people with PhDs, religious people who would pray Salat ul-Layl to people who had just learnt how to pray, from Hawzah students to former communists and so on. In this way, all kinds of people came together in a kind and friendly environment. This battalion contained about forty soldiers. The one thing they had in common was that they all had a high level of morale and bravery. Ibrahim, who had practically taken charge of the battalion would always mention that the battalion didn't have a commander, but he would lead it well through friendship and love. The battalion was organised in such a way that everything that needed to be done would get done without the need for anyone to tell them to do it. Everything would be done by putting their minds together. Ibrahim's right-hand men were Javad Afrasyabi and Reza Goudini.

Every day, the battalion would help the locals and try to resolve their problems, and this would encourage many of the forces from Gilan-e Gharb itself to join the battalion. The main activity of the battalion was to build teams for reconnaissance operations and military operations as well as hiking through the mountains to draw up correct and accurate maps of the enemy's positions.

Ibrahim's strategy of reconnaissance was very strange. He would go into the mountains at midnight with a few others. They would go around the back of the enemy and learn very accurate information of where the enemy is stationed and what their supplies are like. He would say, "If we don't do things like this, we won't know if we will succeed in our operations or not. Therefore, our intelligence must be correct and accurate." Ibrahim also taught his strategies to the other soldiers and he would tell them, "In the matter of reconnaissance, the soldier must be fearless. If the soldier is scared, he will not be successful." He would then talk about how the soldier must have great attention to detail. For this reason, this battalion raised the greatest spies and even commanders in the forces. According to the commander of the 313th Hurr Battalion which oversaw reconnaissance and operations in the Najaf Headquarters, "Ibrahim founded the 313th Hurr Battalion with his special strategies even though he was martyred before it was established."

During its one year of activity, the unorganised troops of the Shaheed Andarzgu Guerrilla Battalion carried out fifty-two major and minor operations. They harassed the Fourth Army Corps of the Iraqi Army in the western provinces and dealt them heavy losses. Great people were made by this small battalion and the era of the Holy Defence is indebted to their sacrifices. They learnt great lessons from Ibrahim and shared in his pride. These people included Shaheed Reza Cheraghi, the brave commander of the 27th Hazrat-e Rasool (s) Division, Shaheed Reza Dastvareh, deputy of the division, Shaheed Hasan Zamani, the organiser of the division, Shaheed Sayyid Abolfazl Kazemi, commander of the Meysam Battalion, Shaheed Reza Goudini, commander of the Honein Battalion, Shaheed Mohammadreza Ali Owsat, undersecretary of the Muslim ibn Aqeel Brigade, Shaheed Darvish Rizehvandi, commander of the Malek Battalion, Shaheed Ibrahim Hesami and Shaheed Hashim Kalhor, undersecretaries of the Meqdad Battalion, Shaheed Javad Afrasyabi and Shaheed Ali Khorramdel, intelligence directors of the division, in addition to many other great commanders of the era of Holy Defence who are still an honour for the Islamic world.

THE MARTYRDOM OF ASGHAR VESALI

Narrator: Ali Moqaddam

In Muharram 1980, an important event took place. Asghar Vesali and Ali Qorbani came to Gilan-e Gharb from Sarpol-e Zahab with their forces. The plan was to start the operation from the north of the city after gaining sufficient intelligence. In those days, the Andarzgu Battalion had just been formed. Only part of the enemy's positions had been discovered.

On the eve of Ashura, all the soldiers gathered in the base, and a beautiful mourning ceremony was held. Many of the soldiers still remember Ibrahim's recitation that night. He was reading with great passion and Asghar was in the middle of all the mourners.

On the Day of Ashura, Asghar went with a few other soldiers to the province of Bar Aftab on a reconnaissance operation. Around noon, there was news that they were ambushed by the Iraqis. The reinforcements hurried over there and pushed the enemy back quickly. However, Ali Qorbani had been martyred and there was no hope in Asghar's survival due to the severity of the wounds he had received. We sent Asghar back to the hospital quickly, but he also joined the caravan of the martyrs.

After Asghar's martyrdom, I saw Ibrahim crying loudly and saying, "Nobody knows what kind of commander we have lost. Our Revolution needed the likes of Asghar." Asghar attained martyrdom in the afternoon of the Day of Ashura, less than forty days after his brother's martyrdom.

Ibrahim came to Tehran for his funeral and brought Asghar's car back to Tehran from Gilan-e Gharb even though the whole car was damaged because of the amount of debris that had hit it. After Shaheed Vesali's funeral, we rushed back to the war provinces. Ibrahim said, "A few nights before his martyrdom, Asghar saw his brother in his dream saying, 'Asghar, you will be martyred in Gilan-e Gharb on Ashura.'" The day after, the soldiers of the battalion held a mourning ceremony for Asghar. The soldiers promised to take revenge for Asghar as long as blood flowed in their veins. Javad Afrasyabi and a few others said, "We will not trim our beards like those who are in mourning until we show Saddam the result of his actions."

A SIMPLE APPEARANCE

Narrator: Some of the martyr's friends

Since the beginning of the war, many of the soldiers had made Ibrahim their role model and took pride in their friendship with him but he would always try to go about his business without attracting attention to himself. For example, he wouldn't wear a military uniform. Instead, he would wear a long shirt and Kurdish trousers. In this manner, he would become closer to the locals and he would also stop himself from becoming proud.

He was simple and ordinary. The first time I saw him, I initially thought he was a janitor for the soldiers, but after a while, I slowly understood what kind of a person he was. He would go against the norms. Rather than focusing on his outer appearance, Ibrahim was more focused on his interior, and everyone would copy him.

He would always say, "More important than keeping

the soldiers in uniforms is that we think about teaching them and keeping up their spirituality so that we can establish friendships with them." The result of such thinking was seen in the performance of the [Shaheed Andarzgu] Battalion's soldiers, though some people were opposed to his ideology.

One day, he bought some camouflage cloth, gave it to a tailor and told him, "Make me a pair of Kurdish clothes." The next day, he picked the clothes up and wore them. He looked very nice in them. He left the base and when he came back an hour later, he returned in army uniform! I asked, "Where are your clothes?" He told me, "One of the Kurdish soldiers liked my clothes so I gave them to him as a gift." He had also given away his watch. That person asked what time it was, and he gave him the watch! These small acts of kindness made many of the local Kurds fall in love with Ibrahim's akhlaq and they eventually joined the Shaheed Andarzgu Battalion.

Despite his simple appearance, Ibrahim was well-versed in political issues and would analyse political events precisely. A little while after we hung up the photos of the late Imam (ra) and Shaheed Beheshti (ra) in the base, the command unit of the west of the country under the supervision of Bani Sadr[75] ordered to cut off all provisions for that battalion and to close it down completely. However, a commander of the Armed Forces in that vicinity announced that the presence of the battalion in the province was necessary as all their attacks were organised and planned by that battalion. They eventually went back on their decision after that commander insisted they do not close the battalion.

One morning, they announced that Bani Sadr wanted to visit Kermanshah. Ibrahim, Javad and a few others went along

---

75   The Iranian president from 1980-81, when he was impeached from his position for anti-revolutionary activities

with Haj Hosein to Kermanshah. The military commanders were waiting for Bani Sadr in neat and tidy clothes, but the soldiers of the Shaheed Andarzgu Battalion came to meet Bani Sadr in their Kurdish trousers, the way they would normally dress, even though they had ulterior motives. They said, "We want to speak with this person and see what kind of military vision he is using to manage this war." We were delayed severely that day, and they eventually announced that the president would not be coming to Kermanshah as his helicopter had been damaged.

A while later, Ayatollah Khamenei came to Kermanshah. At that time, he was the imam of Friday prayers in Tehran. Ibrahim took all the soldiers along to meet him in their simple clothes and they each hugged and kissed him.

THE IMAM HASAN (A) RIVERBANK

Narrator: Hosein Allah-Karam

We were preparing for our first infiltration operation deep behind enemy lines. Ibrahim, Javad Afrasyabi, Reza Dastvareh, Reza Cheraghi and four others were chosen for this operation. Two local Kurds who knew the route well also joined us. We took enough food for a week which mainly consisted of bread and dates. We packed as many weapons, explosives and anti-vehicle mines into our bags and we set off. We travelled through the mountains and Imam Hasan (a) River. We reached its riverbank where an Iraqi military brigade was stationed. We hid in among the valleys and the hills. The enemy didn't think that the Iranian forces would be able to get past these mountains, so for that reason, mapping the area was not too hard.

We stayed in that area for three days. The heavy rainfall did prevent us from our work a little bit but with the hard work of the soldiers, we managed to draw up accurate maps of the area. After completing our intelligence operation and drawing up our maps, we visited the military roads and laid down some anti-vehicle mines. We then started running back towards our base. We had not gotten far when we heard a few explosions. When we looked back, we could see the Iraqi vehicles and APCs in flames.

We quickly fled from the danger. After a few minutes, we realised that the enemy was chasing us with their tanks and infantry. We made our way back to Imam Hasan (a) River through the valleys and hills and once we crossed the river, the enemy could no longer chase us with their tanks. We found a suitable place close to the river, but a few minutes later, we heard a helicopter coming towards us from afar! We hadn't thought of this possibility. Ibrahim immediately put the maps into a bag, handed it over to Reza and said, "Javad and I will stay. Go quickly!" There was nothing else we could do. We gave them our extra ammo and a few grenades, and we left them. The whole operation was to draw up these maps as doing so would increase the chance of success in our future operations. We saw Javad and Ibrahim from afar constantly changing position and firing at the helicopter with their G3 rifles. The Iraqi helicopter was roaming on top of them and raining down on them with bullets.

Two hours later, we reached the mountains. Silence had dominated over the area. One of the soldiers who loved Ibrahim a lot started crying. We didn't know where they were, we didn't know whether they were alive or not. I remembered the day before when we were bored while hiding in the valley, Ibrahim started playing a game with the others. He then started teaching the Kurds in our group some Farsi words. He was so calm that we didn't even feel like we were in enemy territory. When it became prayer time, he wanted to recite the adhan aloud! After we insisted, he read it quietly and then he started praying with a special kind of serenity. During that period, Ibrahim had a kind of bravery which removed the fear from the hearts of the others.

It was night and it had been hours since we last saw Ibrahim. We reached the place where we agreed to meet each other before sunrise and rested for a few hours, but still, there was no sign of them. We needed to leave as the sun was slowly rising. The boys were constantly doing dhikr and reading duas. As we were getting ready to leave, we heard a noise in the distance. We loaded our weapons and took cover. A few minutes later, we recognised the voices; it was Ibrahim and Javad! We were all bursting with joy. The others and I went to help them, and we left the area quickly. The maps that we had drawn up in this infiltration operation proved to be very useful in the next few attacks and we wouldn't have been able to get these maps if it wasn't for the bravery of Ibrahim and Javad.

Noon the next day, Ibrahim and Javad were sitting with the soldiers, ready and full of energy. I went up to Ibrahim with Reza and asked, "Ibrahim, what did you do yesterday when the helicopter came?" Ibrahim replied, "Allah helped us. Javad and I separated from one another and we would constantly change our positions, but we didn't stop shooting. The helicopter would continuously turn around and shoot at us. When the helicopter's ammunition ran out, it returned to its base. We then ran towards the mountains as fast as we could before the other soldiers could arrive. A few small pieces of debris also hit us for us to keep as souvenirs!"

THE PRISONER

Narrators: Mahdi Faridvand, Mortaza Parsaeiyan

Ibrahim would always respect others, even prisoners of war. We would always hear Ibrahim say, "Many of the enemies are ignorant and unaware. They must witness the true Islam from us. Only then will they oppose the Baathist party." For this reason, he would always try to take the enemy captive during our operations before shooting. He was also very kind towards the captives.

Three Iraqi captives had been brought into the city, but there was still no place to keep them. We gave Ibrahim the responsibility of guarding them. Ibrahim would distribute his share of whatever provisions we would get amongst the captives. All of us loved him because of these things, even prisoners. He knew a bit of Arabic so when we had nothing to do, he would go and start a conversation with the prisoners. They were with Ibrahim for two days until the captive transport vehicle arrived. They asked Ibrahim if he was going to go with them and when he said no, they became very upset. They were begging and crying, "Leave us here, we will do whatever you want. We're even willing to fight the Baathists!"

The operation on the Bazi-Deraz Mountains began. I went to the top of the mountains with another person and we slowly moved away from our troops. We came to a trench that was occupied by a few Iraqis. I signalled at them with my gun, telling them to get out the trench. I didn't expect them to be so many! We soon realized they were fifteen people and we were only two. I told them to get moving, but they didn't move a muscle. They surrounded us in such a way that I thought that they were going to attack us. Perhaps they didn't think that we were only two people either. I shouted at them and signalled for them to move again but they didn't. They only did what their high-ranking officer was telling them to do. The Baathist officer lifted his eyebrows as if to tell them not to move. I was terrified. Never had I been in such a situation. I was overwhelmed with fear and I thought to myself, "Maybe I should shoot them all," but that wasn't the right thing to do. The situation was volatile. I gripped my gun with fear and asked Allah to help me. At that moment, I saw Ibrahim coming towards us from behind the trench. I felt relieved.

When he arrived, I shouted to him while watching the captives, "Agha Ibrahim! Help!" He asked what the problem was, and I told him, "The Iraqi officer is the problem. He doesn't want them to move!" His clothes and rank were different to the rest and it was obvious that he was their superior. Ibrahim slung his weapon over his shoulder and went forward. He held the officer's collar with one hand and his belt with the other and picked him up with great ease! He then took him a bit closer to the cliff and held him over it. All the Iraqis sat down and put their hands up. The Iraqi officer was constantly begging Ibrahim not to kill him and asking for mercy. I was no longer afraid. Ibrahim put the officer down next to the other captives. That day, Allah had sent Ibrahim to help me. After that, we brought the prisoners and the Baathist officer down the mountain.

THE 15TH OF SHA'BAN

Narrator: Some of the martyr's friends

Ibrahim entered the base in the afternoon of the 15th of Sha'ban[76]. No one had heard from him since midnight and now he had come back with an Iraqi prisoner. I asked, "Ibrahim, where have you been, who is this prisoner?" He told, "I had gone towards enemy lines at midnight and I hid next to the road. I was watching the Iraqi vehicles pass. When the road became less busy, an Iraqi Jeep which contained one passenger started driving towards me. I ran into the middle of the road, took the Iraqi officer as my prisoner and came back. On the way, I thought to myself, "This is our birthday gift for Imam Mahdi (aj)," but then I became regretful about what I said. I thought to myself, "Who are we to give a gift to Imam Mahdi (aj)!?"

---

76 Birthday of Imam Mahdi (aj)

That day, we all sat around, and we talked about several subjects. Someone asked Ibrahim, "Who do you consider to be the best commanders on the warfront and why?" Ibrahim thought for a bit and then said, "In the IRGC, I don't know anybody like Mohammad Boroujerdi. Mohammad did something nobody was willing to try. Despite all the problems in Kurdistan, he managed to set up Kurdish Muslim Peshmerga groups, thus bringing peace back to the area.

In the Armed Forces, I know no one like Major Ali Sayyad Shirazi. He is even simpler than the volunteer troops. Even before joining the military, Agha Sayyad was a believing and revolutionary youth.

In the Air Force, however, no matter how much you search, you will not find anyone better than Captain Sheeroudi. In Sarpol-e Zahab, Sheeroudi prevented multiple Iraqi counterattacks with his helicopter. Even though he has become the commander of the Air Force, one would be surprised to see how simply he lives. When they brought a few pairs of trainers from the Sports Department, I gave a pair to him because he didn't even have a proper pair of shoes even though he was the commander."

That day, we started talking about our desires. Everyone said something and most of them expressed the desire to attain martyrdom. Some people like Shaheed Abolfazl Kazemi said jokingly, "Allah picks out his good and pure servants. For that reason, I continuously sin so that the angels don't come after me! I want to live for now!" The soldiers laughed and then it was Ibrahim's turn. Everyone was waiting to hear what he wished for. He paused for a bit and then said, "My wish is to be martyred, but not now! I want to be martyred fighting against Israel!"

I came back to Gilan-e Gharb from the trenches early in

the morning but when I entered the IRGC base, there was no one there which wasn't common. I searched a little, but I couldn't find anyone. I became very worried; what if the Iraqis had occupied the city?! "Is there anybody here?" I shouted in the courtyard. One of the soldiers opened a door to one of the rooms and signalled for me to come in. I went into the room and saw that everyone was sitting facing the Qibla quietly. Ibrahim was sitting in the next room on his own and was reciting with great anguish in his voice. He was reciting for himself and he was beseeching Imam Mahdi (aj). There was such pain in his voice that everybody was crying.

THE PRIZE
Narrator: Qasim Shaban

Once one of our infiltration operations came to an end in the west, we sent everyone back on leave. After the end of the operation, we checked each trench to make sure there was no one was left behind. We were the last people to come back.

It was one o'clock in the morning and we were walking back with three others. I said to Ibrahim, "Agha Ibrahim, I'm very tired, let's rest here if it's no problem." Ibrahim agreed, so we chose a suitable place and started to rest. As I was falling asleep, I sensed that someone was approaching us from the enemy's territory. I jumped up straight away and I looked out from the corner. I had guessed right; I could see an Iraqi under the moonlight carrying somebody on his shoulder towards us. I called Ibrahim quietly.

I looked around and I noticed it was just him. The Iraqi was all on his own! When he came quite close to us, we jumped out of the trench and stopped the Iraqi from coming any closer. The Iraqi soldier was terrified and sat where he was. I then realised that he was carrying one of our soldiers who had been wounded and left behind on his shoulders! I was extremely surprised. I slung my gun over my shoulder, and we took the wounded soldier off his shoulders. Reza asked him, "Who are you, what are you doing here?"

The Iraqi soldier replied, "After you left, I was patrolling your trenches and positions when I saw this young boy writhing in pain and calling out for our master Amir al-Mu'mineen (a) and Imam Mahdi (aj). I thought to myself, "Let me leave this youth near the Iranian trenches and come back while it is still dark, and the Baathists still haven't arrived for the sake of our master Ali (a)." He added, "Think of us Shia soldiers who are forced to come to the warfront differently to the Baathist officers." His words had a great effect on me. Ibrahim said to the Iraqi soldier, "If you want, you can stay with us here and not go back. You are our Shia brother." The Iraqi soldier took a photo out of his shirt pocket and said, "This is my family. If I join your forces, Saddam will kill them."

He then stared at Ibrahim's face with surprise. After remaining quiet for a few moments, he said in Arabic, "You are Ibrahim Hadi!" We were all stunned into silence! We were all looking at one another surprised. This sentence needed no translation. Ibrahim asked with a smile from surprise, "How do you know my name?" I joked with Ibrahim, "Agha Ibrahim, you didn't tell us that you had friends among the Iraqis!" The Iraqi soldier explained, "A month ago, they had sent your picture along with a few other commanders to every military unit and told us, 'Whoever brings the head of one of these Iranian commanders will receive a big prize from Saddam!'"

In those days, we learnt that the IRGC command unit in the west had sent a director for the Shaheed Andarzgu Battalion and that he was on his way to Gilan-e Gharb to take responsibility. We waited but no director arrived until one day, we were informed that Jamal Tajeek, who had been serving in our battalion as a regular soldier for a while, was the director we were looking for. Ibrahim, a few others and I went to Jamal and asked him, "Why didn't you introduce yourself?! Why didn't you tell us that you were the director of the battalion?". He looked at us and said, "My responsibilities include making sure that work is getting done. Thank God, work is being carried out in the best manner here. I also enjoy myself when I'm with you, and I'm grateful to Allah that I got to know you. Don't tell anyone because then people might start acting differently with me." A while after, Jamal was martyred in Operation Matla' al-Fajr[77] while serving as the commander of the shock troop battalions.

ABU JA'FAR

Narrator: Hosein Allah-Karam, Farajollah Moradiyan

At the beginning of 1981, news arrived that another operation had been carried out on the Bazi-Deraz Mountains. The soldiers of the Shaheed Andarzgu Battalion were chosen to carry out infiltration operations behind enemy lines. For this operation, Vahab Qambari[78], Reza Goudini and I were chosen in addition to Ibrahim. Two Kurds from the province, Shahrokh Nooraei and Heshmat Kuh-Peykar also joined us. We took some important provisions such as food, weapons and a few anti-vehicle mines.

When it became dark, we set off for the mountains. Once we passed through the mountains, we reached the Dasht-e Gilan Province. As the sun rose, we set up in a suitable place and concealed ourselves. As well as resting during the day, we also

---

77 عملیات مطلع الفجر
78 Vahab Qambari was one of the founders of the army in Kermanshah and one of the local Kurds. He had completed university and had memorized both the Qur'an and Nahj al-Balaghah. Most of the soldiers believed that it was only due to his bravery that the riots in Kurdistan were subdued. Vahab received the reward for his hard work and was martyred.

identified the enemy positions and the roads running through the plains. We also drew a map of the enemy's positions. The plain in front of us had two roads, one made of asphalt and one track which was made through the sand which was only used for the military activity. These two roads were approximately five kilometres away from each other. A company of Iraqi soldiers which was stationed at the top of the hill and the sides of the roads was tasked with maintaining the security of the region.

Once night fell, we set off after praying. Reza Goudini and I went to the asphalt road and the rest went to the desert road. We took cover on the side of the road and when there were no cars, we quickly ran onto the road. We laid two anti-vehicle mines inside the potholes. We covered them with sand and then we ran towards the sand road. It was clear from the movement of the enemy forces that they were still fighting in the mountains. Most of the Iraqi forces and vehicles were travelling away from their base. On our way towards the desert road, we heard a formidable explosion from behind us. We both took cover and looked back. An Iraqi tank had driven over a mine and was on fire. A few moments later, the missiles inside the tank also started exploding one by one. The fire from the tank had illuminated the whole area. The Iraqi guards were terrified, and they started to shoot without a target.

When we reached Ibrahim and the others, they had also done what they needed to do so we set off towards the mountains. Ibrahim said, "There's a lot of time left until sunrise and we have a lot of weapons and ammo. Come, let's frighten them even more by setting up ambushes." Before Ibrahim finished his sentence, we heard an explosion from the sand road. An Iraqi vehicle had driven over the mine and had been destroyed. We were all glad that the operation had been a success.

The Iraqis started shooting even more as they realised that we had infiltrated the area. For this reason, they started firing mortar shells and flares, so we rushed towards the mountains.

There was a hill in front of us. Suddenly, an Iraqi Jeep came out from behind it and it was heading towards us. It was so close; we didn't have enough time to make a decision. We quickly took cover and started shooting at the Jeep. A few moments later, we went towards the Iraqi vehicle. We had killed a high-ranking Iraqi officer and his chauffeur. A radioman was laying on the ground, wounded. A bullet had hit his leg and he was constantly crying in pain. One of the soldiers cocked his gun and went towards the radioman. The youth was constantly crying, "Have mercy, have mercy!" Suddenly, Ibrahim shouted, "What do you think you are doing?" The soldier replied, "Nothing, I want to put him out of his misery." Ibrahim replied, "My friend, he was our enemy when we were shooting, but now he is at our mercy, he is our prisoner." He then went towards the Iraqi radioman and picked him up off the ground. He put him on his back and started moving. Everybody was watching Ibrahim's conduct with great surprise. One person asked, "Ibrahim, do you know what you are doing? We have to walk thirteen kilometres through the mountains just to reach our positions." Ibrahim turned back and said, "Allah gave me a strong body for these kinds of days."

He then started moving towards the mountains. We quickly took the equipment from the Jeep including the Iraqi radio and started moving again. We rested for a bit and bandaged the Iraqi's leg wound at the bottom of the mountain, and then we continued walking. After seven hours of hiking, we reached the front line. Ibrahim was talking with the Iraqi captive on the way who was in turn, constantly thanking Ibrahim. At the time of Fajr, we prayed in congregation in a safe place. The Iraqi captive also prayed in congregation with us! It was then that we realised he was also a Shia. After praying, we ate some food and we distributed everything we had among us equally, including the captive. The prisoner didn't expect us to be so kind. He introduced himself, saying, "My name is Abu Ja'far, I'm a Shia and I live in Karbala. I didn't think you would behave like this with me, etc." He told us a lot, but we only managed to understand a few words.

We reached the Bansiran Cave before the sun rose fully, so we rested there and sent Reza Goudini towards our forces to bring help. An hour later, Reza came with vehicles and reinforcements and called us. I asked, "Reza, what's up?" He replied, "When I was coming back to the cave, I became worried as I saw an armed person sitting in front of the cave. At first, I thought it was one of you but when I came closer, I saw Abu Ja'far, the Iraqi captive, guarding the cave while carrying a gun. As soon as I saw him, the colour drained from my face, but he said salaam and gave me the weapon. He then said in Arabic, "Your friends were asleep when I noticed the Iraqi patrol passing by. That's why I came out to stand guard so that if they came any closer, I could shoot them!"

We went back to the base with the others and Abu Ja'far stayed with us for a few days. Ibrahim went to the hospital because of the weight he carried on the way. Ibrahim returned a few days later, and everyone was pleased to see him. I called him over and told him, "The IRGC command unit in the west have come to thank you." He asked why and I told him, "Come with me and you will know!" I took Ibrahim to the IRGC base, and one of the directors said, "Abu Ja'far, the Iraqi prisoner that you brought with you, was the radioman of the base of the 4th Iraqi Division. The intel that he gave us about the formation of the troops, the positions of the battalions, the commanders and the routes of infiltration is of great, great value." He added, "This prisoner has been speaking for three days and all his information is correct. He has been in this region since the first day of the war. He has even told us about all the Iraqi infiltration routes and the radio codes they use. It is for this reason we have come to thank you for this great service of yours." Ibrahim smiled and said, "Come on, what have I done?! This was Allah's work!"

The next day, they sent Abu Ja'far to the POW camp. Ibrahim

tried a lot to let Abu Ja'far stay with us, but they didn't allow it. Abu Ja'far said, "I beg you, please keep me here. I want to fight against the Iraqis!" but they didn't accept.

A while later, I heard that a group of Iraqi prisoners had established a battalion called the Tawwabeen[79] Battalion and had come to the warfront. They fought against the Iraqis alongside the soldiers of the Badr Brigade.

In the afternoon, one of my old friends from the Shaheed Andarzgu Battalion came to visit me and he said cheerfully, "I have something interesting to tell you. Abu Ja'far, that Iraqi prisoner, is working in the base of the Badr Brigade."

There was an operation soon so after the operation was completed, I went to the Badr Brigade's base with a few friends. We agreed that we would do everything we could to bring Abu Ja'far to our battalion. Before entering the main building of the base, we witnessed a scene which was difficult for us to believe. The photos of the martyrs of the brigade were on display on the wall, and Abu Ja'far's photo was among the martyrs of the Badr Brigade's latest operation. My head felt light and I felt strange. I was looking at his photo with great wonder. We didn't enter the main building and we left the brigade's base. I started thinking about the memories from that night; the attack on the enemy, Ibrahim's self-sacrifice, the Iraqi radioman, the POW camp, the Badr Brigade, and then martyrdom. Lucky for him!

---

79   Meaning 'the repentant'

THE FRIEND

Narrator: Mostafa Harandi

He was very restless, and sorrow could be seen on his face. I asked if something had happened to which Ibrahim replied sadly, "We had gone on an intelligence operation with a few others. On our way back, MashaAllah Azizi[80] stepped on a mine right next to the enemy lines and was martyred. The Iraqis started to shoot, and we were forced to come back [and leave his body there]." I had only then realised why he was sad.

At sunset, Ibrahim set off and when he returned in the middle of the night, he was overjoyed. He was constantly shouting, "Medic! Medic! Come quickly, MashaAllah is alive!" Everyone was glad and we put MashaAllah Azizi into the ambulance, but Ibrahim sat in a corner, deep in thought. I sat next to him and asked him, "What are you thinking about?" He replied, "MashaAllah had fallen in the middle of a minefield near the Iraqi trenches. However, when I went to look for him, he wasn't there. I found him closer to our trenches, in a safe place far from the enemy. He was sitting there waiting for me."

"I had lost a lot of blood from my leg and I had become numb. However, the Iraqis were certain that I was dead. Under my breath, I was constantly calling out to Imam Mahdi (aj) for help. When it became dark, a handsome young man with a bright face came and stood above my head. I opened my eyes with difficulty. He picked me up very carefully and took me out of the minefield. He put me down on the ground in a safe place slowly and calmly. I didn't feel any pain at all! That man had a full conversation with me and then he said, "Somebody will come and save you. He is our friend!" A

---

80   MashaAllah Azizi was one of the sincere and God-wary soldiers of Gilan-e Gharb

few moments later, Ibrahim arrived, put me on his shoulder and brought me back. That young man had introduced Ibrahim as his friend. Lucky for him!"

MashaAllah had written this in his memoir notebook in Gilan-e Gharb.

MashaAllah stayed in the region for a few years. He was one of the great role models of sincerity and God-wariness in Gilan-e Gharb who took part in all operations on the warfront from the first day of the war until the last. After the war, he joined his martyred comrades in a car accident.

LOST AT WAR

Narrator: Mostafa Harandi

He returned before the adhan of Fajr with the body of a martyr on his shoulder. Exhaustion was visible on his face. In the morning, he took a leave of absence and then we left with the martyr's body. Ibrahim was tired but glad. He said, "A month ago, we carried out an operation on the Bazi-Deraz Mountains. Only this martyr's body was left behind. Once the area calmed down, Allah helped us, and we managed to bring him back." News reached Tehran very quickly. Everyone was waiting for the martyr's body, and a glorious funeral was held from Khorasan Square the next day. We wanted to stay in Tehran for a few more days, but we were informed that another operation was underway and so, we decided to leave the night after from the mosque.

I was standing outside the mosque with Ibrahim and a few others after prayers. As we were speaking and laughing, an elderly man walked up to us. I recognised him. He was the father of the martyr, the same martyr whose body Ibrahim had brought from the mountains. We said salaam and he answered our salaam. We all went quiet. It was as if he wanted to say something, but something was stopping him. A few moments later, he broke the silence and said, "Agha Ibrahim, thank you. You struggled a lot, but my son..." The old man paused and then continued, "My son is unhappy with you!"

The smile was wiped off Ibrahim's ever-smiling face and his eyes bulged in surprise. Why?! He had a lump in his throat and his eyes welled up with tears. He said, his voice shaky and weak, "Last night, I saw my son in a dream. He said to me, 'When my body was lost at war[81] and I was laying on the ground on the warfront without any marker, the mother of the Imams, Lady Fatimah (a) would visit us every night, but now, there is no such thing." He said, "Those martyrs whose bodies are lost at war are the special guests of Lady Fatimah (a).'" The old man didn't go on any longer. We were all stunned into silence. I looked at Ibrahim and I saw teardrops falling from the corners of his eyes. I read his mind; he had found his long-lost love: being lost at war!

After that incident, Ibrahim's outlook on the war and the martyrs changed a lot. He would say, "I have no doubt anymore that the martyrs of our war are no less than the followers of Prophet Muhammad (s) and Imam Ali (a). Their position in the eyes of Allah is very high." I heard him say many times, "If somebody has a wish to be with Imam Husayn (a) in Karbala, the time to test

---

81 Whenever we talk about 'lost at war', it means that they have been martyred but their bodies hadn't been recovered

yourself has arrived." Ibrahim was certain that one could attain eternal happiness and perfection through the Holy Defence. For this reason, he would speak about the martyrs wherever he went, and he would praise the soldiers and commanders of the war. His mannerisms were changing day by day and he was becoming more spiritual.

During the time we were at the base of the Shaheed Andarzgu Battalion, he would sleep for one or two hours at night and then he would go outside. He would come back at the time for Fajr and would wake the soldiers up for prayers. I thought to myself, "Ibrahim hasn't been sleeping here for a while!"

One night, I followed him, and I noticed that he went to the base's kitchen to sleep. The next day, I spoke with an old man who worked in the kitchen and I learnt that all the kitchen staff pray Salat ul-Layl. For this reason, Ibrahim went out because if he stayed inside, everybody would find out that he prayed Salat ul-Layl. These actions and Ibrahim's conduct reminded me of Imam Ali (a)'s narration in which he said to Nawf Bakāli, "My Shias are those who are worshippers at night and are lions in the day."

ONLY FOR ALLAH
Narrator: One of the martyr's friends

I went to see one of my friends whose foot had been severely injured during an operation in the west. As soon as he saw me, his face lit up and he started thanking me a lot. I didn't understand the reason for his excessive appreciation. He said, "Sayyid dear, I'm sorry I put you through a lot of trouble. If you hadn't brought me back, I would have been taken captive!" I asked, "Do you know what you are talking about? I left the warfront with the provisions vehicle before the rest of the other troops and went on leave." He replied with surprise, "No man, it was you, you helped me and bandaged the wound on my leg." However much I insisted that I didn't do it, he wouldn't believe me.

A while passed, I thought about what my friend said again and suddenly, I thought of something. I went straight to Ibrahim. He was also involved in that operation and had also come back on leave. I took him to my friend's house and told him, "The person you have to thank is Agha Ibrahim, not myself because I am not the kind of person to carry someone else back for eight kilometres, especially through mountainous terrain. That's how I figured out who it must have been! A person who doesn't speak a lot, has the same physique and upper body strength as me, and also knows me. I figured it must have been him!" However, Ibrahim didn't say anything. I said, "Agha Ibrahim, I swear by my grandfather[82] that if you don't say anything, I will be annoyed with you!" but Ibrahim was angry with me because of what I had done. He replied, "Sayyid, what shall I say?" He paused for a bit, and then continued calmly, "I was going back empty-handed and I saw that he had fallen in a corner. There was no one behind me. I was the last person. I stopped the bleeding from the wound on his leg with my bootlaces in the darkness and continued onwards. He was calling me Sayyid on the way, so I realised he must be one of your friends. That's why I didn't say anything until we reached the medics."

Ibrahim was very angry at me after that and didn't talk to me for a few days. I understood why; he would always say that something done in the way of Allah does not need to be spoken about.

We infiltrated enemy positions with the rest of our spies. As we were busy exploring the area, we noticed that there was

---

82 All Sayyids are descendants of the Prophet (s) through his daughter Lady Fatimah (a), so he is swearing by the Prophet (s)

a herd of sheep nearby. The shepherd came and said salaam. He then asked, "Are you Khomeini's soldiers?" Ibrahim went forward and answered, "We are Allah's servants." He then asked, "Father, what are you doing in these mountains and valleys?" The shepherd replied, "I live here." He then asked, "Have you faced any problems?" The old man smiled and replied, "I would have already left had there been no problems." Ibrahim gave the old man a box of dates, some bread and some provisions and said, "This is a gift to you from Imam Khomeini." The shepherd was delighted, prayed for us and then we went on our way. Some of the others started to protest, saying, "We have to stay in this region for a week and you gave most of our provisions to this old man!" Ibrahim replied, "Firstly, it is not clear how long our work will take. Secondly, I assure you that this shepherd will never be our enemy. Have no doubt that every action performed in the way of Allah will never go without a reward." In that operation, we did our work very quickly despite the lack of provisions and we even ended up with excess provisions.

IN THE PRESENCE OF THE GREAT

Narrator: Amir Monjar

During the first year of the war, I came back on leave. I was going from Sarasyab Square towards Khorasan Square on my motorcycle with Ibrahim sitting on the back. As we passed by a street, Ibrahim quickly told me to stop. I stopped as fast as I could on the side of the road and asked, "What happened?!" He replied, "Nothing. If you have time, let's go and visit someone." I said, "Okay, I'm not doing anything right now."

Ibrahim and I entered a house and we went into a room after calling out 'Ya Allah' a few times. A few people were sitting down in the presence of an old man with a black cloak who was sitting at the front. We said salaam and sat in a corner of the room. Once the Haj Agha finished his conversation with one of the youths, he turned towards us and said smiling, "Agha Ibrahim, have you lost your way? You hardly visit anymore!" Ibrahim lowered his head and replied respectfully, "I'm ashamed Haj Agha, I don't have any time to come." It was clear from the way they talked to each other that he knew Ibrahim well. Haj Agha spoke with the others for a bit and once everyone left, he turned to Ibrahim and said humbly, "Agha Ibrahim, please give me some advice!" Ibrahim went red with embarrassment, raised his head and said, "Haj Agha, please don't embarrass me. Please don't speak in this manner." He added, "We came to visit you and Insha'Allah we will attend to your weekly gathering." We then got up, bade farewell and left.

On the way back, I said, "Ibrahim dear, you could have advised him a little bit, you don't need to go red in the face!" He interrupted me and said angrily, "What are you talking about, dear Amir? Do you even know who that man was?!" I replied, "No, who was he by the way?" Ibrahim replied, "This man is one of those drawn close to Allah, but many people don't know him. He was Haj Mirza Ismaeel Dulabi." Many years passed until people started to know of Haj Agha Dulabi. Only when I read his book 'The Blessing of Love' did I realise the greatness of the sentence he said to Ibrahim.

One of the most important operations in the west of the country came to an end and after some coordination, many of the soldiers went back to Tehran to visit Imam Khomeini (ra). Despite the important role Ibrahim played during the operation, Ibrahim didn't go back to Tehran. I went and asked him, "Why didn't you go?" He replied, "The warfront must never be empty of soldiers, some must always stay behind." I asked, "Was that the reason you didn't go?" He thought a little and elaborated, "We don't want a leader who is just for visiting, we want a leader to obey." He added, "It's not important for me to see my leader. What is important rather is that we obey his commands and that my leader is content with what I am doing."

Wilayat ul-Faqih[83] was a very sensitive subject for Ibrahim, and he also held strong opinions about Imam Khomeini (ra). He would say, "No great person nor scholar, contemporary or of old, ever had the courage and passion of Imam Khomeini." Whenever a speech of the late Imam (ra) would be broadcast, he would listen carefully and say, "If we want both this world and the next, we must act upon the words of the Imam." Since his youth, Ibrahim was very close to the scholars of his neighbourhood. He benefited greatly from Allamah Ja'fari during the time he lived in our neighbourhood. He also considered Shaheed Ayatollah Beheshti and Shaheed Ayatollah Motahhari[84] to be complete role models for the younger generation.

ZIYARAH

Narrators: Jabbar Setoudeh, Mahdi Faridvand

In the first year of the war, I went to one of the mountain ranges north of Gilan-e Gharb with the soldiers of the Andarzgu Battalion. We were stationed atop one of the hills facing the border in the early morning. The border had been occupied by the Iraqis and their vehicles were passing through the roads with no difficulties. Ibrahim opened a supplication booklet and we recited Ziyarah Ashura together. Afterwards, I looked down at the regions occupied by the enemy forlornly and said, "Ibrahim dear, look at

---

83   Guardianship of the Jurist
84   Ayatollah Mortada Motahhari was one of the leading figures and thinkers of the Revolution. He is considered as one of the top scholars of philosophy and epistemology today. He was martyred after being shot on the 1st of May 1979 by members of the terrorist Furqan Group.

this road going through the border. The Iraqis are driving through it so comfortably." I continued, still sad, "Do you think one day our people will be able to use this road to go to their cities comfortably?" [I thought] Ibrahim wasn't paying attention to what I was saying, it was as if he was in his own world! He smiled and replied, "What are you talking about? A day will come when our people will use this very road to go to Karbala in groups again!" On the way back, I asked the others about the name of the border and one of them told me that it was called the Khosravi Border.

Twenty years later, I went to Karbala. My eyes fell upon the same mountain on which Ibrahim had recited Ziyarah Ashura. I felt as if Ibrahim was seeing me off. The mountain was directly opposite the Khosravi Border. That day, the buses were on their way to the border and our people were going for ziyarah of Karbala in groups through that route.

Whenever we were in Tehran, Ibrahim would visit the shrine of Shah Abd ul-Azeem Hasani (a)[85] every Thursday night. He would say, "Thursday nights are the nights of Allah's blessings. It is the special night to visit Imam Husayn (a). All of those drawn close to Allah and the angels go to Karbala tonight and I go to a place which has the same virtue as visiting Karbala according to the Ahlulbayt (ams)." He would recite Dua Kumayl there and return at one o'clock in the morning. When the revolutionary youth gatherings were set up, he would come straight to the programme after ziyarah to meet with the revolutionary youth.

---

85   Shah Abd ul-Azeem Hasani was a scholar from the progeny of Imam Hasan (a). He was one of the companions of Imam Rida, Imam Jawad and Imam Hadi (ams). It is narrated that visiting his grave has the same virtue as visiting the grave of Imam Husayn (a).

One night, Ibrahim and I left the shrine together. Since I was in a rush, I borrowed one of my friend's motorcycles and went to the mosque. However, Ibrahim reached the mosque two or three hours later. I asked, "Ibrahim dear, why are you late?" He explained, "I walked from the shrine to visit the grave of Shaykh Sadooq[86]. The old legends of Tehran say that Imam Mahdi (aj) visits his grave on Thursday nights." I asked, "Well, why did you walk?" He didn't give a proper answer, so I asked again, "You were in a rush to reach the mosque earlier, but you walked it. There must have been a reason!" After I insisted for a bit, he admitted, "As I was leaving the shrine, an extremely destitute person came and asked me for money, so I took a handful of money out of my pocket and gave it to him, but when I was about to get into a taxi, I realised that I didn't have any money. That's why I walked."

Towards the end [of our time together], we would sometimes go to Behesht-e Zahra to visit the martyrs after visiting the shrine of Shah Abd ul-Azeem every week. Ibrahim would then recite for all of us. On some nights, he would sit inside a grave. He would recite Dua Kumayl with great pain in his voice and he would mourn.

THE GRENADE
Narrator: Ali Moqaddam

Before Operation Matla' al-Fajr, a meeting was held between the commanders of the IRGC and the Armed Forces at the base of the Shaheed Andarzgu Battalion. The meeting's objective was to achieve greater cooperation between the different branches

---

86   Abu Ja'far Muhammad ibn 'Ali ibn Babawayh al-Qummi, also known as Shaykh Sadooq, was one of the most prominent scholars of Shia faith, and compiled many famous books such as Man La Yahduruhu al-Faqeeh and al-Khisal.

involved in the operation. Apart from myself and Ibrahim, there were three commanders from the Armed Forces and three commanders from the IRGC present in the meeting. Meanwhile, a few other soldiers were busy carrying out military training in the courtyard.

As we were all busy discussing our tactics, suddenly, a grenade flew through the window and landed exactly in the centre of the room! The blood drained from my face. I took cover by crouching beside the wall, my head cradled between my hands. I was so afraid, I couldn't breathe. The others had also taken refuge in the other corners of the room like me. The moments passed in fear, but we didn't hear an explosion! I peeked towards the middle of the room from between my fingers, and I saw something hard to believe. I took my hands off my head slowly. I raised my head, looked with awe and exclaimed, "Agha Ibrahim...!" The others also slowly started to get up from their corners. Everyone looked towards the centre of the room, the blood slowly returning to their faces. Contrary to us who had taken cover in every nook and cranny, Ibrahim had run and laid down on top of the grenade!

At that moment, the military trainer entered, apologised and said, "I'm so sorry, it's only a training grenade, it was thrown into the room by accident." Ibrahim got up off the grenade. Since it was only the first year of the war, none of us had ever experienced something like this. It was as if this grenade had been thrown into the room to test our courage. From then on, everyone was talking about the story of the grenade.

OPERATION MATLA' AL-FAJR

Narrator: Hosein Allah-Karam

A while after Bani Sadr was impeached, a chain of operations was organised on the northern, western and southern warfronts to bring the Iraqi army to its knees. On the 28th of November, the first major operation by the name of 'Tariq al-Quds[87]' was launched and we dealt the first substantial blow to the forces of the Baathist Party.

According to the command unit, the second operation was to take place in Gilan-e Gharb Province, specifically in Sarpol-e Zahab which was the nearest warfront to the city of Baghdad. For this reason, our troops had been spying on the area to find out details about the enemy's preparations from a while back. The responsibility of this operation lied on the shoulders of the IRGC command unit in Gilan-e Gharb. All the members of the Andarzgu Battalion were putting in an extra shift to get all the necessary tasks done on time. Ibrahim was tasked with spying on the enemy troops. He carried out this matter with precision and accuracy in a very short amount of time. Ibrahim took one of the Kurds with him beyond enemy lines to collect the intelligence, and in a matter of one week, they managed to complete reconnaissance until Naft Shahr. In this space of time, Ibrahim managed to draw accurate maps of the area, and he returned to the base with four Iraqis who he had taken captive. After interrogating the captives and learning valuable information, he completed the maps for the operation and presented them in a meeting with the command unit.

Colonel Ali Yari and Major Salami from the Dhul-Fiqar Brigade of the Armed Forces coordinated with the IRGC as well. Many of the local troops from Sarpol-e Zahab and Gilan-e Gharb were also organised into battalions. Most of the soldiers from the Shaheed Andarzgu Battalion were chosen as the commanders of these battalions. A few battalions from the IRGC and the volunteer forces were chosen as the shock troops. They were given the duty of launching the operation.

In the final meeting, the command unit appointed Ibrahim as the commander of the centre of the warfront, Brother Safar

---

[87] Meaning 'The Road to Jerusalem', the aim of this operation was to liberate the city of Bostan

Khoshravan as the commander of the left-wing and Brother Darvish Rizehvandi as the commander of the right-wing of the operation. The objectives of the operation were to liberate the mountains overlooking Gilan-e Gharb from enemy troops and to liberate the mountains on the border, the Hajiyan and Gurak Valleys and the sentry posts along the border. The operational region almost exceeded seventy kilometres. We received word from the base that straight after our operation, a third offence would be launched on Mariwan.

Everything was being coordinated. A few days before the launch, the command unit of the army announced, "Iraq has prepared a huge counter-attack to reoccupy the city of Bostan. You must launch the operation as soon as possible to distract the Iraqis from the city of Bostan." For this reason, the next day i.e. the 11th of December 1981 as the day on which we would launch the operation. There was a strange atmosphere [in the barracks]; we were about to launch the first large-scale operation in the west of the country and on the mountains. No one knew what could happen so everybody in the barracks bade farewell to each other in case this was their last meeting.

Finally, the promised day arrived. Many important and strategic areas such as the Hajiyan and Gurak Valleys, the village of Bar Aftab, and the mountain ranges of Sartatan, Charmiyan, Dizehkesh, Fereydoun Houshyar, as well as parts of the Shiyakouh Mountain Range and all of the villages surrounding Dasht-e Gilan were liberated by our simultaneous widespread assaults.

On the main front, the forces liberated a few hills and rivers and advanced until the Pomegranate Hills from which the enemies were raining fire upon us relentlessly. A few battalions were able to pass the hill and they reached the Shiyakouh Mountain Range. Some had even reached the top of the mountains. The enemy knew that losing the Shiyakouh Mountain Range meant losing the Iraqi city of Khanaqin. Hence, they sent more reinforcements towards the mountains and the battlefield.

Around midnight, we were informed via radio that Hasan Balash and Jamal Tajeek had reached the Shiyakouh Mountain Range with their forces and had requested reinforcements. A few moments later, Ibrahim called and said, "All of the Pomegranate Mountains have been liberated, there's just one strategically well-positioned hill that is putting up heavy resistance. We also don't have many troops." I told Ibrahim, "I'll join you before sunrise with the reinforcements. In the meantime, coordinate with the commanders of the Armed Forces and put all your effort in liberating that hill." I moved towards the central warfront with one auxiliary battalion. On the way, the IRGC command unit announced, "The enemy has cancelled their counterattack on the city of Bostan, but they have moved many of their troops from there to your front. Resist and Insha'Allah, the army of Mariwan under the command of Haj Ahmad Motevaselian will start the next operation soon." They also thanked the soldiers of the IRGC and the Armed Forces for the well-coordinated attack and said, "According to the reports we have received, Iraq suffered heavy losses on your front, and the command unit of the Iraqi army has ordered in more reinforcements."

It was nearing sunrise, so we stopped on the way to pray Fajr. As we were approaching the Pomegranate Hills, we were met with the news of the martyrdom of Gholam-Ali Pichak on the Gilan-e Gharb warfront. As soon as we reached the Pomegranate Hills, one of the soldiers came up to us and said in his Mashhadi accent, "Haj Hosein, have you heard that they shot Ibrahim?" I felt shivers down my spine, and I asked him what had happened. He replied, "A bullet hit Ibrahim in his neck." My face went pale and I felt lightheaded. I started running towards the trenches in front of me. On the way, I saw all my memories with Ibrahim flash before my eyes. I entered the medical trench. A bullet had struck the muscles in Ibrahim's neck and he had lost a lot of blood. I found Javad and asked him, "What happened to Ibrahim?!" He paused a little and replied, "I don't know what to say." I asked, "What do you mean?!" He explained, "We spoke with the commander of the Armed Forces and asked how to attack the hill. The Iraqis were showing heavy resistance. They had a lot of troops stationed on and around the hill. Everything we tried bore no result. It was almost the time of Fajr, and we needed to do something, but we didn't know what that something was. Suddenly, Ibrahim left the trench! He walked towards the Iraqis' hill, stood on a boulder and faced the Qibla. He started reciting the adhan for Fajr loudly! We were shouting for him to come down and that the Iraqis were going to shoot him, but he wasn't listening. He had almost completed the adhan. We were surprised to see that the Iraqis had reduced their fire, but just at that moment, a bullet was fired, and it struck Ibrahim. We then brought him back."

MIRACLE OF THE ADHAN

Narrator: Hosein Allah-Karam

We were in the Pomegranate Hills and the sun had completely risen. The medic had bandaged Ibrahim's neck wound. I was busy dividing the troops and answering the radio. Suddenly, one of the soldiers came running and said, "Haji, Haji, a few Iraqis are coming this way with their hands up!" I asked him where they were, and we went to a trench opposite the hill. Around twenty people were coming towards us waving a white flag. I said right away, "Arm yourselves, it might be a trap!" A few moments later, seventeen Iraqis led by their commanding officer surrendered themselves. I was happy that despite the hostile atmosphere, we had managed to take these Iraqis captive. I thought to myself that the brave assaults of the soldiers and the execution of the operation must have scared them into captivity.

I brought the highest-ranking Iraqi into the trench and I called one of the soldiers who knew Arabic over. Like an interrogator, I asked him, "What's your name, tell me your rank and post as well!" He introduced himself, saying, "I'm a major and the commander of the troops stationed on and around the hill. We are from the reserve army of Basra and we were dispatched to this region." I asked, "How many troops are stationed on the hill right now?" and he replied, "As of right now, none!" I couldn't believe my ears! "None?!" I exclaimed. He replied, "We came to surrender ourselves, and I sent the rest of the troops back. Now the hill is empty." I asked him the reason and he replied, "Because they didn't want to surrender." I asked why again and instead of answering, he asked, "Where is the muezzin?!" I asked, "Muezzin?" His eyes welled up with tears and he started speaking with a lump in his throat:

"They told us that you were Magus and fire-worshippers. They told us that we are attacking Iran and fighting the Iranians for Islam. Believe me, we are all Shia. When we saw that our commanders drink alcohol and don't pray, we doubted whether we should go to war. This morning, when we heard your soldier reciting the adhan loudly, I felt shivers down my spine. When he mentioned the name of Amir ul-Mu'mineen (a), I thought to myself, 'You are fighting against your own brothers. What if this war is like that of Karbala?!" His tears didn't allow him to finish his sentence.

A few minutes later, he continued, "For this reason, I decided to surrender and not add to my sins. I ordered a ceasefire. Once the day dawned, I gathered the troops and told them that I wanted to surrender to the Iranians and whoever wanted could come with me. These people who have come with me all have the same beliefs as me. All the other forces went back. Of course, I also brought the soldier who shot at the muezzin. If you give me the order, I will kill him. Now please tell me, is the muezzin alive or not?!" I was listening to what the Iraqi commander was saying stunned. I had no reply. After a few moments of silence, I told him, "Yes, he is alive."

We left the trench together and went to Ibrahim who was sleeping in one of the other trenches. Each of the eighteen Iraqi captives came and kissed Ibrahim's hand. The last person fell crying at Ibrahim's feet and said, "Forgive me, I was the one who shot!" I felt as if I was about to cry. The atmosphere was strange. My attention was no longer on the operation. As I was about to send the Iraqi captives back, the Iraqi commander called me over and said, "Look over there. One commando battalion and a few tanks are ready to advance from there." He added, "Go quickly and occupy the hill." I immediately sent a few members of the Andarzgu Battalion towards the hill. Once the mountain was liberated, the whole region was finally back under our control.

The commando battalion did attack, but because we were prepared for it, most of their forces were killed and the attack was deemed unsuccessful. In the following days after Operation Mohammad Rasulullah (s) in Mariwan, the amount of pressure the Iraqi army was putting on Gilan-e Gharb lessened.

Operation Matla' al-Fajr achieved many of its objectives and liberated many regions of our dear country despite the loss of exceptional commanders such as Gholam-Ali Pichak, Jamal Tajeek, Hasan Balash and others. A few days later, Ibrahim re-joined the battalion after recovering fully. That day, it was announced, "In the Operation Matla' al-Fajr which had the holy codeword *'Ya Mahdi (aj), adrikni!'*[88], more than fourteen battalions of Iraqi special forces were eliminated. Their losses included two thousand killed and wounded and two hundred Iraqis taken captive. Also, two fleets of Iraqi warplanes shot down."

---

[88] Arabic for 'come to my aid'

Five years passed since Operation Matla' al-Fajr. We were carrying out Operation Karbala 5 in Shalamcheh in the winter of 1987. Part of the responsibility of coordinating with the divisions and reconnaissance for the mission was put on my shoulders. I went to the base of the Badr Brigade to coordinate with them and brief them as they were to take part in the next stage of the operation. The brigade was made up of soldiers who spoke Arabic and Iraqis who were against Saddam. After talking with the commanders of the division and the commanders of the battalions, I managed to coordinate with them successfully and I got ready to leave.

I noticed one of the soldiers of the Badr Brigade staring at me and then he came closer. As I was getting ready to leave, the soldier came up to me and said salaam. I replied to his salaam and then he said in an Arabic accent without introduction, "Weren't you in Gilan-e Gharb?" I said yes. I thought he was one of the soldiers from the west. He continued, "Do you remember Operation Matla' al-Fajr? The Pomegranate Hills, the last hill!" I thought a little and then asked, "What about it?" He replied, "Do you remember the eighteen Iraqi soldiers that were taken captive?" I said, "Yes, who are you?" He said happily, "I'm one of them!" I was surprised! I asked him what he was doing there, and he explained, "All eighteen of us are in this battalion. We were freed after Ayatollah Hakeem became our guarantor. He knows us well. Hence, we decided to come here to fight the Baathists!" This was all very strange to me. I said, "May Allah bless you. Where is your commander?" He replied, "He has a post in this battalion. Now we're advancing towards the front line together." I told him, "Write your names and the name of your battalion on this piece of paper, I'm in a rush right now. I'll come here after the operation and meet you all properly." While he was writing their names, he asked, "What was the name of the muezzin?" I replied, "Ibrahim, Ibrahim Hadi." He said, "We have all been looking for him for such a long time. We even asked our commanders to find him for us. We would love to see that man of

God again." I went quiet and I felt a lump grow in my throat. He raised his head to look at me and I told him, "Insha'Allah you'll see each other in Paradise." He became extremely sad because of that. He wrote the names and the name of his battalion and gave them to me. I quickly bade farewell and left. This unexpected meeting left a great impact on me.

The operation was completed in March 1987 and many of the troops went back on leave. One day as I was going through my belongings, I found the piece of paper on which the Iraqi wrote his details. I went searching for the soldiers of the Badr Brigade. I asked one of the commanders about the battalion, but he replied, "This battalion has been disbanded." I said, "I want to meet the members of the battalion." The commander elaborated, "The battalion you are talking about resisted against a heavy Iraqi counter-attack in Shalamcheh with the commander of the division. They suffered great losses, but they didn't retreat." He paused for a few moments and then continued, "No one from this battalion came back alive!" I said, "These eighteen people were some Iraqi prisoners. Their names are here, and I came here to meet them." He came, took the paper and gave it to somebody else. A few minutes later, that person came back and said, "All of these people have been martyred!" I didn't know what to say. I sat down and started to think. I thought to myself, "Ibrahim achieved so much with one adhan! A hill was liberated, an operation succeeded and like Hurr[89], eighteen people were saved from the depths of Hell and entered Paradise."

I then remembered what I had said to that Iraqi soldier, "Insha'Allah you'll see each other in Paradise." I started crying uncontrollably. I bade farewell and went outside. I had no doubt that Ibrahim knew the right time and place to recite the adhan to strike fear into the hearts of the enemy and to guide the people who had some faith remaining in their hearts!

---

89   Hurr ibn Yazid ar-Riyahi was one of the commanders of Yazid's army until the 10th of Muharram. He was the one who stopped Imam Husayn (a) in Karbala, but after the Imam (a)'s speech, his conscience awoke, he turned repentant and defected to the Imam (a)'s side.

THE SCARVES

Narrator: Abbas Hadi

Ibrahim was back on leave at the beginning of 1982. He got home in the middle of the night and we spoke a little bit. I noticed that he had a large amount of money in his pockets, so I asked, "By the way, where do you get so much money from? I've seen you help people and even spend money on religious programmes so many times, but you still have so much money in your pocket!" I then said jokingly, "Tell me the truth, have you found treasure?" Ibrahim laughed and said, "No man, my friends give me the money and they tell me how to spend it."

The next day, I went to the bazaar with Ibrahim. We passed by a few shops and stalls until we reached a specific shop. It was a relatively big shop. From the way the old man who owned the shop and his apprentices shook Ibrahim's hand and hugged him one by one, it was clear that they knew him well. After exchanging pleasantries, Ibrahim said, "Haji, I will be leaving for Gilan-e Gharb tomorrow Insha'Allah." The elderly man replied, "Ibrahim dear, do you need anything for the soldiers?" Ibrahim took a piece of paper out of his pocket, gave it to the elderly man and said, "As well as these few things, we also need a video camera. The courage and heroics of our troops must be recorded. Those who come after us must know how our religion and country was defended." He then added, "We also need a lot of scarves for the soldiers."[90] The shopkeeper's son came forward when he heard what Ibrahim said and asked, "I understand why you would need a video camera, but Ibrahim, why would you need scarves? Do you want to put on bandanas like the gangsters?" Ibrahim answered, "Look, my brother, a scarf is not a bandana. Whenever the soldiers do wudu, the scarf is a towel for them, whenever they pray, it is a prayer mat, whenever they are wounded, it is a bandage and…" The old

---

[90] Whenever we mention scarves, we are referring to the chequered kind of scarves which are normally black and white

man who owned the shop interrupted him and said, "Sure, Agha Ibrahim, we will get them for you too."

The next day before noon, the old man came with a pickup truck filled with equipment as I was standing outside the house. I rushed into the house and called Ibrahim. The old man gave Ibrahim a camera and a few other things and said, "Ibrahim dear, the pickup truck is filled with scarves for you."

A while after, Ibrahim explained how much those scarves helped in Operation Fath ol-Mobin.[91] Slowly thereafter, using scarves became a part of the uniform of the warriors of Islam.

SENSE OF HUMOUR
Narrators: Ali Sadiqi, Akbar Nowjavan

During times where he needed to be serious, Ibrahim would act very professionally. However, outside of work time, he was very witty and good company. This was one of the reasons that many people were enchanted by Ibrahim.

Ibrahim had a special etiquette when eating food. Whenever there was enough food, he would eat well. "My body needs food more due to my activities and exercise," he used to say. Once, Ibrahim went to a traditional Iranian breakfast shop with one of our local friends from Gilan-e Gharb in Kermanshah. They both managed to eat three servings!

---

91 عملیات فتح المبین

Another example is when one of his friends invited him over for lunch. He fried six chickens for three people and prepared a large amount of rice and of course, nothing was left over!

I went to visit Ibrahim when he was wounded. We then went to one of our friends' houses with a motorcycle to open our fast. The host was one of Ibrahim's close friends. He was also very insistent on us having food. On the other hand, Ibrahim didn't require a second invitation. He ate as much as he could, and there was nothing left on the dinner spread by the end.

One of our friends, Ja'far Jangravi, was there too. After opening our fast, he was continuously going into the adjacent room and calling his friends. He would bring them into the room one by one and say, "Ibrahim dear, this person wants to meet you." Ibrahim was forced to stand up out of respect every time even though he had eaten a lot and his foot was hurting due to his wound. Meanwhile, Ja'far stood behind them laughing quietly. Whenever Ibrahim would sit, Ja'far would go and bring the next person. He did this a few times until Ibrahim told him calmly, "My dear Ja'far, I will get you back for this!"

We decided to leave at midnight. Ibrahim got on the bike and told me to drive quickly. Ja'far also got on his bike and started following us. Eventually, we fell quite far ahead of him. As we approached a checkpoint, I came to a halt. Ibrahim called out loudly, "Brother, come here!" One of the armed youths came, and Ibrahim explained, "Look, my dear friend, I'm a veteran and my driver is one of the soldiers of the IRGC. There is a motorcycle following us which..." Ibrahim paused and then continued, "It's better if I don't say anything. Just be very careful. I think he's armed!" We then said goodbye and continued on our way. I drove a little further and then parked on the pavement. We both just started laughing.

When Ja'far arrived, four armed people surrounded his motorcycle. Once they found his pistol, they disregarded anything he had to say. Around half an hour later, the manager of the checkpoint arrived and recognised Haj Ja'far. He apologised and said to his group, "This is Haj Ja'far Jangravi, one of the commanding officers of the Sayyid ash-Shuhada (a) Division." The soldiers were embarrassed asked for forgiveness. Ja'far was enraged. He collected his weapon without speaking a word, got on his bike and left. When he came closer, he saw Ibrahim standing on the pavement dying of laughter. Only then did he realise what had happened. Ibrahim went and hugged and kissed Ja'far. Ja'far calmed down and he even started to laugh. Thank God that everything ended in laughter.

THE TWO BROTHERS

Narrator: Ali Sadiqi

I went to one of the border cities to attend Shaheed Shahbazi's mourning ceremony. According to the customs and culture of that area, the ceremony continues from morning until noon, when they bring a pitcher and a pot for the attendees to wash their hands to get ready for lunch. When I entered the ceremony, I saw Javad sitting at the front and Ibrahim was sitting next to him. I joined them and sat next to Ibrahim. Ibrahim and Javad were very close friends and they were like two brothers. The way they would joke with one another was interesting in its own way.

At the end of the ceremony, two of the hosts brought the pitcher and the pot, and the first person they went to was Javad. Ibrahim whispered something in Javad's ear. He didn't know much about the customs of the area. Javad exclaimed loudly, "Are you serious?!" Ibrahim replied quietly, "Quiet, don't say anything!" Ibrahim then turned to face me. He was laughing quietly so I said to him, "What happened, Ibrahim? It's wrong, don't laugh!" He explained, "I told Javad that when they bring the pitcher, he should wash his head well!"

A few moments later, that exact thing happened. After

washing his hands, Javad decided to give his head a good wash. He then started looking around in surprise as the water was dripping from his head and face. "What have you done, Javad?!" I asked, "Does this place look like a bath to you?!" I then gave him my scarf to dry his head.

One day, we were informed that Ibrahim, Javad and Reza Goudini were returning to our post on the border from an operation. We were glad that they were returning unscathed and we all gathered outside of the Shaheed Andarzgu Base. A few minutes later, their vehicle arrived, and Ibrahim and Reza got out. The soldiers gathered around them and greeted them cheerfully.

One of the soldiers asked, "Agha Ibrahim, where's Javad?" Everyone went silent instantly, and Ibrahim said sadly as if he was about to cry, "Javad!" He then slowly turned towards the back of the car. Someone was laying there with a blanket over his body. Ibrahim continued, "Javad... Javad!" as tears fell from his eyes. A few of the soldiers started crying and calling Javad's name as they went towards the back of the car. Suddenly, Javad jumped up from his sleep! He sat up and asked, "What? What's happening?" Javad started looking at his surroundings bewildered. The soldiers started looking for Ibrahim, angry and tearful, but he had quickly gone into the building!

THE PISTOLS

Narrator: Amir Monjar

It was almost the end of March 1982. After gathering all our equipment and returning the weapons, we were ready to set off for the south. According to the orders from the commanding unit, a major operation was being planned in Khuzestan and for this reason, most of the IRGC troops and the volunteers were being transferred to the south. The Andarzgu Battalion was also

sent south along with the IRGC soldiers stationed in Gilan-e Gharb.

Towards the end [of our stay in Tehran], the IRGC in Kermanshah announced, "Brother Ibrahim Hadi has taken a crate of Colt pistols and still hasn't returned it." Ibrahim insisted that he didn't have it, but they didn't believe him. "Ibrahim, maybe you took it and forgot to return it," I suggested. He thought a little and replied, "I remember taking it, but I gave it to Mohammad and told him to bring it back and give it in. Mohammad came back to Tehran a week ago." He then asked around and confirmed that the weapon was still in Mohammad's hands and he hadn't given it in.

We went to Tehran and visited his house, but we were told that he had returned to his village by the name of Kuhpayeh, which was off the Isfahan-Yazd Highway. Ibrahim gave a lot of importance to returning weapons, so he said, "Come, let's go to Kuhpayeh." We set off for Isfahan at night and made our way to Kuhpayeh from there. We reached there in the early morning and it was a bit cold. I asked Ibrahim, "So where do we go now?" He replied, "Allah will help us, He will show us the way Himself." We drove around the village for a bit and we saw an old woman going home. She was staring at us as we were not residents of the village. Ibrahim got out of the car and said loudly, "Salaam, mother!" The old lady replied kindly, "Salaam my dear, are you looking for somebody?" Ibrahim asked, "Mother, do you know Mohammad Kuhpayi?" She asked back, "Which Mohammad?" He elaborated, "The one who has recently returned from the warfront, he's about twenty years old." The old lady smiled, told us to follow her and she went to her house.

Ibrahim told me to park the car and then we went together. The old lady invited us in, made us breakfast and said, "You are the soldiers of Islam; eat so that you may become strong." She then continued, "Mohammad is my grandson and he lives in my house, but he has gone to the city and will not be back until night." Ibrahim said, "Sorry mother, your grandson has done something which has brought us here from the warfront!" The old lady looked surprised and asked what he had done. Ibrahim continued, "He took a Colt pistol from me, but he brought it with him here without returning it. They are now telling me that I must return it immediately." The old lady got up and replied, "I don't know what to do with this boy!" Ibrahim said, "Mother, don't worry, we won't bother you for long."

The old lady told us to follow her and took us to a room. She said, "All of Mohammad's belongings are in this closet. A few days ago, I saw him bring something and put it in here. Now you can break the lock yourself." Ibrahim said, "Mother, it isn't right to go through someone else's belongings!" The old lady replied, "I would break it on my own if I was able to." She then went and brought a screwdriver. By levering it, I managed to break the small lock on the closet. When the closet door opened, the pistol was sitting there on his belongings in plain sight covered in a white cloth. I picked up the gun and came out. As we were leaving, Ibrahim asked, "Mother, why did you trust us?" The old lady replied, "The soldiers of Islam don't lie. Would you lie with such radiant faces?"

We made our way to Tehran. On the Isfahan Ring Road, my eyes fell upon the Armed Forces' fire support base. "Agha Ibrahim," I asked, "Do you remember the commander of the Armed Forces' fire support base who was very helpful during our operations in Sarpol-e Zahab?" He replied, "Are you talking about Agha Maddah?" and I said, "Yes, he's now the commander of the Isfahan fire support base. He might be here now." He replied, "Alright, let's go meet him." We pulled up outside the base and I parked the car. Ibrahim got out, went to the guard post and asked, "Salaam, is Agha Maddah here?" The guard looked at Ibrahim from top to bottom; a man wearing Kurdish trousers, a baggy shirt and a simple-looking face had just asked about the commander of the base! I came forward and explained, "My brother, we are Agha Maddah's friends and we have come from the warfront. We'd like to see him if possible." The guard made a phone call and described us. Minutes later, two Jeeps came towards the gate from the command headquarters. As soon as Colonel Maddah saw us, he hugged and kissed Ibrahim. After hugging and kissing me, he insisted on bringing us to the command office. He then took us to the meeting room where around twenty military commanders were currently in a meeting. Agha Maddah was leading the meeting. He brought two chairs for us, sat us down beside the members at the meeting, and then started speaking:

"My friends, all of you know me. Whether it was during the nine-day war before the Revolution or during the first year of the imposed war, I have been awarded promotions and medals of gallantry. The soldiers of my fire support base carry out the most difficult of tasks in the finest manner possible and have been successful in all their operations. I have also undergone all the most difficult and important kinds of military training, both in this country and abroad. However, there have been and are people who put all my military education under question.

For example, the universal rules of war state that if you are attacking a place where the enemy has stationed one hundred units, you must have three hundred units and more provisions to be victorious. This man, Agha Hadi and his friends, have done truly remarkable things. For example, they launched an attack with less than one hundred soldiers but the number of losses the opposition suffered was greater than the number of soldiers they attacked with. I was their support during that operation. I remember well that once, when they wanted to attack the Bazi-Deraz Province and

I saw the state our troops were in, I said to my friend, "They will be defeated." However, I witnessed myself that in this operation, as well as liberating the positions occupied by the enemy, they inflicted more losses on the enemy than the original number of soldiers they attacked with."

One of the young officers present in the meeting said, "Well, Agha Hadi, please explain how you run your operations so that we can learn from you." Ibrahim replied, his head lowered, "No, my brother, we didn't do anything. Agha Maddah has praised us a lot, but we didn't do anything. These were all Allah's blessings." Agha Maddah said, "What he and his friends taught us was that ammunition and the number of troops don't matter. What matters most is the morale of the forces. With one takbeer[92], they struck such fear into the hearts of the enemy which had a greater effect than hundreds of mortar shells and tanks." He continued, "They had a friend who was small in stature, but great in power and bravery. His name was Asghar Vesali who prevented the advance of the enemy with his forces at the beginning of the war and was martyred. It was from these sincere youth that I understood the verse of the Qur'an, "If there are twenty from amongst you who are patient and steadfast, they will overcome two hundred."

An hour later, we excused ourselves from the meeting. We apologised to the members of the meeting and left for Tehran. On the way, I was thinking about what had transpired that day. Ibrahim handed in the gun and we set off for Khuzestan along with the soldiers of the Andarzgu Battalion.

A fourteen-month period in Gilan-e Gharb ended with all its good and bad memories, a period in which great heroism was displayed; a period in which three armoured Iraqi brigades were destroyed by a small group of guerrilla soldiers.

---

92   Saying 'Allahu Akbar'

OPERATION FATH OL-MOBIN

Narrator: Some of the martyr's friends

When we reached Khuzestan, we first went to the city of Shush to visit the grave of Prophet Danyal (a). We were informed there that all the volunteer troops, who are now known as baseejis, had been divided into military brigades and battalions and were getting ready for a major operation. Whilst we were doing ziyarah, we saw Haj Ali Fazli. He welcomed us very warmly and gladly. Haj Ali took us to the al-Mahdi (aj) Brigade, which contained several battalions of baseeji forces and several battalions of soldiers while explaining to us how the troops were distributed.

Haj Hosein [Allah-Karam] had also divided the members of the Andarzgu Battalion amongst the other battalions. Most of these members took the responsibility of intelligence and reconnaissance. Reza Goudini, Javad Afrasyabi and Ibrahim were all put into different battalions. The troops were prepared very quickly. The spies of the IRGC had been working in this area for months. The entire territory currently under the occupation of the enemy was under surveillance and they had even identified where the Iraqi battalions and armoured brigades were stationed.

On the 21st of March 1982, Operation Fath ol-Mobin was launched with the codeword 'Ya Zahra (a)'. That afternoon, the undersecretaries and heads of the battalions were sent to the operational region by the IRGC, and they were giving orders and strategic advice from a far distance. One of the most difficult roles of the mission was given to the battalions of the al-Mahdi (aj) Brigade. As the sun set on the 21st of March, the troops started to get excited. The troops began their advance after prayers.

I didn't leave Ibrahim's side for even a second. Eventually, our battalion started advancing but for different reasons, he and I stayed behind. We finally advanced at two in the morning. In the darkness of the night, we reached our battalion which was sitting in the middle of the field. Ibrahim asked, "What are you doing here?! You're supposed to attack the enemy!" They replied, "It's the commander's orders." We went forward and he asked the commander, "Why have you left them in the middle of the field? The sun is rising, these people neither have cover nor trenches, they are completely within reach of enemy fire." The commander replied, "There's a minefield in front of us and we don't have a bomb disposal officer. We have called the headquarters and one is on his way." Ibrahim said, "There's no time to wait," and then he turned to the soldiers and ordered, "A few self-sacrificing soldiers come with me to open the way!" A few soldiers ran up to him and followed Ibrahim into the minefield. He was dragging his foot on the ground and walking through, the rest doing the same. I was watching Ibrahim in amazement. I couldn't breathe out of fear. The blood had drained from my face. I was expecting the sound of an explosion and Ibrahim's martyrdom at any moment. Seconds felt like hours. However, they managed to reach the other side! Thank God that this field's mines had not been activated.

After passing through the minefield, we attacked the enemy trenches that night and regained some territory. However, we didn't advance too far forward. Close to sunrise, Ibrahim was wounded by a piece of debris which struck his flank and so, the soldiers sent him back. Later that morning, they wanted to send Ibrahim to one of the neighbouring cities by aeroplane. However, after strong insistence, he got out of the plane, got his wound stitched and bandaged in the clinic and returned to the frontline. During the attack on the first night, the commander and vice-commanders of our battalion were wounded. Thus, Ali Movahhed was appointed as the commander of our battalion.

That day, a meeting was held for the commanders including Mohsen Vezvaei to inform them about the next stage of the operation. The essential objective of the next stage was to capture the enemy's heavy fire support base and to pass the Rofaeiyeh Bridge. The reconnaissance wing of the IRGC had been working on this plan for a while. The success of the future stages depended on victory in this stage.

At night, the troops started advancing again. The bomb disposal troops advanced in front of the rest of the troops followed by Ali Movahhed, Ibrahim and the others. Despite walking for a very long time, we never reached the enemy's trenches or fire support base. After walking for six kilometres, we fell, exhausted in the middle of a field. Ali Movahhed and Ibrahim went here and there, but there was no trace of this fire support base. We were lost in a plain behind enemy lines!

There was still a very calm atmosphere among the soldiers. It was so calm that almost all of us fell asleep for half an hour! A while later, Ibrahim said in an interview with the Message of the Revolution Magazine for its March 1982 edition, "That night and in that desert, however much we searched, we couldn't find anything except for more plains. So, we immediately went down into prostration and stayed in that position for a few minutes. We asked Allah to show us the way by the right of Lady Fatimah and the Infallible Imams (ams)." He continued, "In that desert, it was only us and Imam Mahdi (aj), so we called out to him and asked him for help. We didn't know what to do. The only thing we could think of was to call him to help us."

No one knows what happened that night or what words were exchanged between them and Allah in that long prostration, but minutes later, Ibrahim got up and started walking towards the left of where our troops were resting in the plain. After walking for about one kilometre, he reached a large trench. When he looked beyond the trench, he could see many mortar shells and heavy weaponry. The Iraqi soldiers were resting completely peacefully and only a few guards were patrolling the courtyard.

Ibrahim returned to the battalion quickly and told Ali Movahhed what he had seen. They took the soldiers to the trench. On the way there, they advised the soldiers not to shoot until they were ordered and to take as many prisoners as possible. From the other side, the Habeeb Battalion under the command of Mohsen Vezvaei attacked the Iraqi fire support base. That night, we captured the Iraqi fire support base with the least amount of fighting and just by our cries of 'Allahu Akbar' and 'Ya Zahra (a)!' We also managed to take a great number of Iraqis captive. Capturing the fire support base meant that the Iraqi Army would face serious problems in Khuzestan. Our troops quickly turned the artillery guns back towards Iraq, but we didn't use them as none of our troops had the sufficient training.

The fire support base was captured, and we started clearing the region of enemy forces. A few minutes later, I saw Ibrahim bringing an Iraqi officer along with him. He handed the officer over to the soldiers of the battalion. I asked, "Ibrahim, who was he?" He replied, "I was patrolling the perimeter of the base and, suddenly, I saw this officer coming towards me. The poor man didn't know that we liberated the entire area. I told him to surrender, but he attacked me. He didn't have a gun, so I wrestled with him and threw him to the ground, then I tied his hands and brought him here."

We prayed Fajr outside the fire support base, and as the reinforcements arrived, we continued advancing on the plain. The area in front of us had not been completely cleared of enemy forces yet. Suddenly, two Iraqi tanks came towards us, but they turned around and retreated. Ibrahim quickly ran after one of the tanks, jumped on top of it, opened the hatch and said something in Arabic. The tank stopped, and a few workers jumped out, declaring their surrender.

As the sun rose, the troops were arranged, and we started our advance. On the way, I asked Ibrahim, "Did you notice that we attacked the enemy's fire support base from behind?" Ibrahim asked, "No, why though?" I replied, "The enemy was waiting for us at the front with a lot of soldiers, but Allah inspired us to go from another way so that we could attack the enemy from behind. That's why we were able to take so many captives and find so many provisions. The enemy was completely ready for our attack until two in the morning. That's when they started resting and we attacked at that moment." We gathered the captives again and we sent them back with a few soldiers. We then set off with the rest of the troops for the final stage of the operation.

WOUNDED

Narrators: Mortaza Parsaeiyan, Ali Moqaddam

All the battalions advanced from their positions. We were supposed to pass through the area and its surrounding trenches ahead of us. However, this became a lot more difficult as the sun rose. Our job became especially difficult in an area close to the Rofaeiyeh Bridge. An Iraqi soldier was firing a sentry gun from a bunker and he wasn't allowing any of our troops to pass. Despite our best efforts, we couldn't even touch him in his concrete bunker.

I called Ibrahim and pointed towards the soldier's bunker from afar. He looked carefully and said, "The only option we have is to get closer and throw a grenade into the bunker." He then took two grenades from me and crawled towards the enemy trenches. I followed him as well. I took cover in one of the trenches, but Ibrahim went a bit further and I sat there watching. He had taken up a good position near the soldier, but something strange happened. There was a young baseeji in that trench who was traumatised. He was constantly shouting, "I'll kill you, Iraqi!" and he gave his AK-47 to

Ibrahim. As Ibrahim was sitting, he raised his hands and didn't say anything. Neither I nor anybody else dared to breathe. We didn't know what to do. A few seconds passed, the sound of the machine gun not stopping even for a second. I started crawling forwards and I managed to reach that trench. I was constantly praying, "O' Allah, help us! We haven't faced any problems since last night, but now we're stuck in this situation!"

Suddenly, Ibrahim hit the baseeji on his face and took his gun from him. After that, he hugged the baseeji! The youth, who had come back to his senses, started crying. Ibrahim called me over, told me to look after the baseeji soldier and said, "I have never punched anybody's face before this, but right now, it was needed." He then went closer to the Iraqi soldier. A few moments later, he threw the first grenade but to no avail. He then got up and ran outside the trench, throwing the grenade whilst running. A moment later, the machine gunner's bunker was destroyed.

All the soldiers got up while chanting 'Allahu Akbar' and started advancing. I was watching them with great joy. Suddenly, one of the soldiers signalled to me so I turned around and looked outside the trench. The blood drained from my face and the smile was wiped off my face; Ibrahim was laying on the floor, drenched in blood. I threw my gun to the side and ran to him. At exactly the moment of the explosion, a bullet had hit his face [the back of his mouth] and another had struck the back of his foot. He had lost a lot of blood and he was lying on the floor, almost unconscious.

With the help of one of the other soldiers, we sent Ibrahim and a few other wounded soldiers in a vehicle to a military hospital in Dezful. Ibrahim was involved in all stages of the operation and right at the end when we were liberating the final enemy trenches in that area, he was wounded. I couldn't stop crying on the way. I was scared that Ibrahim wouldn't make it. He had also lost a lot of blood when he was wounded on the first night of the operation and now, it was not clear if he would be able to make it.

The medic in Dezful said, "A bullet hit his face but miraculously, it came out through his neck without doing any damage. On the other hand, the bullet which hit his foot has taken away the ability to move it and his heel bone is fractured. Also, the stitches on the wound on his flank have opened and it is now bleeding. Therefore, he must be transferred to Tehran to be examined."

Ibrahim was transferred to Tehran and admitted to Najmiyyeh Hospital for a month. They operated on him several times and they also removed a few small and large pieces of debris from his body. In an interview with a journalist who had come to meet him in the hospital, he said, "Even though the soldiers put in a lot of hard work for months for this operation, Allah showed us His blessings, we didn't do anything in Operation Fath ol-Mobin! We were only guided, and our motto was 'Ya Zahra (a)!' Whatever happened there was from the inspiration of Lady Zahra (a)." He continued, "When we took the soldiers here and there in the desert and everyone was tired, I went into prostration and I asked Imam Mahdi (aj) for his intercession. I asked him to show us the way. When I lifted my head from prostration, I noticed a strange kind of calmness had descended upon the soldiers and most of them were asleep. A cool breeze was also blowing so I moved in the direction it was blowing. I only walked for a little bit when I stumbled upon the trenches surrounding the fire support base." In the end, the journalist asked, "Do you have a message for the people?" He replied, "We are embarrassed to look these people in the eye who don't eat dinner so they can send it to the soldiers. I have to be torn into pieces so that I can compensate for their sacrifices!"

Ibrahim was unable to walk as his heel bone was fractured. He came home after staying in the hospital for a little while and he was kept from the warfront for around six months. However, he continued his social and religious activities with the youth in his neighbourhood and the mosque.

RECITATION

Narrators: Amir Monjar, Javad Shirazi

When Ibrahim was in high school, he established the Islamic Unity Youth Organisation with his friends. He was a source of goodness for many of his friends. Many times, he would advise his friends to continue establishing religious programmes in our neighbourhoods to safeguard their religious spirit. He also emphasised that the programmes must revolve around a lecture.

One of his friends narrates, "A few years after Ibrahim's martyrdom, I was organising cultural programmes in one of the mosques of Tehran. One day, I was wondering how we could establish and uphold a relationship between the youth and the mosque's cultural activities. That night, I saw Ibrahim in a dream. He had gathered all the youth from the mosque and said, "Protect the youth by organising weekly programmes!" and then he explained how to do so. I organised them exactly how he told he explained. At first, I thought it was not going to work, but after many years, the relationship between those youth and the mosque is still strong."

He would behave the same way with the youth in the neighbourhood. After drawing them towards the gym, he would then encourage them to attend the mosque and he would say, "Once the youth put their hands in the hands of Imam Husayn (a), the problems will be resolved. He will guide them."

Since high school, Ibrahim started reciting for Imam Husayn (a) and he would also encourage the others to do so too. Every week, he would recite for the Islamic Unity Organisation with Shaheed Abdullah Masgar. This was more than just any another organisation; it had a profound effect on the theological and even political beliefs of the youth. They would invite scholars such as Allamah Mohammad Taqi Jafri and Haj Agha Najafi and some other religious and political personalities to deliver speeches. As a result, the SAVAK held this organisation under close supervision and prevented their gatherings from taking place a few times.

Ibrahim began reciting in this organisation and the gym while doing *Varzesh-e Bastani*. His voice reached perfection during the Revolution and beyond. However, he would always observe the following point, "I read for my own heart. I try to benefit from the recitation more for myself and I try to not have other un-godly intentions while reciting."

He was sitting on the motorcycle and he started to recite poems about Lady Zahra (a) in a beautiful tune. There was a lot of love in his voice and I asked Ibrahim to read the same poem that night in the programme in the same style. He refused despite my insistence and he kept saying, "They already have a reciter. I don't have a nice voice either, so keep dreaming!" However, I knew that he would always refrain from doing things which may lead to un-godly actions or cause him to be mentioned by others.

Ibrahim had interesting habits when reciting in a gathering. He didn't need a microphone or echo to recite and he recited without a microphone many times. He would beat his chest firmly and say, "The Ahlulbayt (ams) gave their entire existence for Islam, we should at least beat our chests well for them." He would recite wherever he saw he had a duty to do so, be it in a wedding or a mourning ceremony. However, if he realised there was another reciter, he wouldn't recite, and he would benefit from the recitation. Ibrahim was the embodiment of the narration from Imam Rida (a), "Whosoever cries upon our calamities and makes others cry even if it is only one person, his reward is with Allah. Whoever cries while listening to the calamities which befell us, Allah will resurrect him with us."[93]

He would adopt a reverent state during the mourning

---

[93] Mustadrak al-Wasa'il, vol. 1, p. 386

ceremonies, and many would become rejuvenated when they saw him like this. Wherever he went, Ibrahim would make that place feel like Karbala. A good example of this was Arbaeen 1982 in a gathering organised by the Asheqan-e Hosein Committee. The members of the committee will never forget that day. Ibrahim was reciting about the calamities that befell Lady Zaynab (a) and became so overwhelmed that he fell unconscious! That day, there was such a spiritual atmosphere, one I am sure I will never witness ever again. I'm certain that this atmosphere only came about due to Ibrahim's passion and love in his voice.

Ibrahim had many interesting views on recitation. He would say, "The reciter must protect the Ahlulbayt (ams)'s reputation whilst reciting, he mustn't just say anything. He mustn't recite about the calamities which befell the Ahlulbayt (ams) if he can see that the gathering isn't appropriate for it." Ibrahim never considered himself a reciter, but wherever he recited, he would create a great passion among the people. He would never forget to mention the martyrs, and he wrote a few couplets of poetry with the names of the martyrs in it, especially Asghar Vesali and Ali Qorbani, which he would recite in the gatherings.

It was the night before *Tasu'a*[94] and a large mourning ceremony was held in the mosque. At first, Ibrahim was beating his chest well, but I didn't see him again after that! He was standing in a corner under the darkness of the gathering and beating his chest quietly. The programme went on for some time and it ended at midnight. When it was time for dinner, everybody gathered around Ibrahim and I said, "It was a very amazing session, everybody did very well." Ibrahim took a meaningful look at us and said, "Keep your love to yourselves!" When he saw our surprised faces, he

---

94   The 9th day of Muharram

continued, "These people had come to mourn for Abbas (a), to ensure their love for another year. When the programme goes on for a while, they become tired. Give people their food after some mourning, and then after that, mourn and express your love to the Ahlulbayt (ams) to your heart's content. Don't let the people get tired because of the programmes of the Ahlulbayt (ams)."

THE MAJLIS OF LADY FATIMAH (A)

Narrator: Some of the martyr's friends

We went to a gathering of reciters at the Haj Abol-Fath Mosque. Many poems were recited in this gathering about the virtues of Lady Fatimah (a) and Ibrahim was writing them down. At the end of the gathering, Haj Ali Insani started reciting about the calamities that befell Lady Fatimah (a) and Ibrahim fell into a state of extreme sorrow. He put his booklet of poems down and started crying loudly. Once the gathering ended, we left for home. On the way, he said, "When one attends a gathering about Lady Fatimah (a), he must feel her presence as this gatherig is about her."

One night, we went to a programme celebrating Eid az-Zahra (a)[95] after I insisted for him to come. I thought that Ibrahim would be excited because he loved Lady Fatimah (a) very much. The reciter was using bad words as if to make Lady Fatimah (a) happy. Halfway through the programme, Ibrahim signalled to me and we left.

On the way, I asked, "I think you're angry, right?" Ibrahim looked at me while shaking his hands out of anger and said, "There

---

95   Eid az-Zahra (a) is the day that Imam Mahdi (aj) was appointed as an Imam

is no sign of Allah in these programmes. Always go to places where they speak about Allah and the Ahlulbayt (ams)." He repeated this sentence several times. A while later, when I heard the views of the scholars about these kinds of programmes and the importance of protecting unity among the Muslims, I understood how much insight Ibrahim had.

When Ibrahim was injured during Operation Fath ol-Mobin, we immediately transferred him to the military hospital in Dezful. There were many wounded soldiers admitted to the hospital. The hall was very busy. The wounded were all crying out and it was as if there was no peace and quiet whatsoever. We eventually managed to find a space and we laid Ibrahim down. The nurses bandaged the wounds on his neck and foot.

All the wounded were crying out in pain. In such conditions where there was no sign of peace and quiet, a place filled with injured soldiers, Ibrahim started reciting very loudly. He recited a very beautiful poem about the virtues of Lady Fatimah (a) whose blessed name was the codeword of the operation. For those few minutes, the whole place went quiet. No wounded soldier even made a sound. It almost felt as if everything had returned to normal. Wherever I looked, everyone was completely calm. Teardrops were rolling down the faces of both the wounded and the nurses.

Once Ibrahim finished, a nurse who was older than the others and didn't wear proper hijab came forward. She seemed very affected by the poem, and said quietly, "You're just like my son! May I be sacrificed for you, you youth!" She then sat and kissed Ibrahim on the forehead. Ibrahim's face was very funny to watch at that moment. His ears had gone red, he pulled the covers over his face out of embarrassment.

Ibrahim would always say, "After trusting in Allah, seeking intercession from the Infallibles (ams), especially Lady Fatimah (a), will always solve your problems."

We went to Najmiyyeh Hospital to visit Ibrahim and we sat with him. Ibrahim took permission and then started to recite about the calamities that befell Lady Fatimah (a). Two doctors came and were watching him from a distance. I asked if anything had happened and they replied, "No, we were on the plane with him. He would go in and out of consciousness, but he would continuously recite about Lady Fatimah (a)'s virtues in a beautiful voice."

THE SUMMER OF '82

Narrator: Mortaza Parsaeiyan

Ibrahim was forced to remain in Tehran for the summer of 1982 due to his wounds. He started working in the Education and Training Department. He completed many military courses while working, as well as organising several cultural programmes. He did all this work in such a short time!

He was going up and down the stairs of the Education and Training Department on crutches. I went to him and said salaam. I asked, "Agha Ibrahim, what happened? If you need to do something, tell me so I can help you." He replied, "No, I'll do it myself." He then went to several rooms and gathered a few signatures.

When he finished what he was doing, I asked him as he was leaving the building, "What was that letter? Why were you bothering yourself so much over it?" He explained, "Somebody has been a teacher for two years, but hasn't been able to find a job yet. I sorted it out for him." I asked if he was from the warfront and he replied, "I don't think so, but he asked me to do this for him. I came here because I realised that I could help him out." He added, "One must do as much as he can for the servants of Allah, especially for the good people we have. We must do whatever we can for them. Have you not heard the Imam say that the people are the custodians of our blessings?"

Everyone in the neighbourhood knew Ibrahim. They would be captivated by his personality and principles the first time they would meet him. Ibrahim's friends were always at his house. When the soldiers would come back from the warfront, they would visit Ibrahim before going to their own houses.

One morning, the imam of the Muhammadiyah Mosque didn't come. The people sent Ibrahim forward after insisting a lot and they prayed behind him. When the imam heard, he was overjoyed and stated, "If I was there, I would have also been proud to pray behind Agha Hadi."

I saw Ibrahim walking down the road on crutches. Every so often, he would glance at the sky then look down. I went and asked him what had happened. At first, he didn't reply, but after I insisted, he explained, "Every day until now, somebody would have come to me by this time and asked me to help them however I could. However, no one has come to me since the morning. I'm worried that Allah has taken away the blessing of being able to help His servants from me!"

THE METHOD OF NURTURING

Narrators: Javad Majlisi-Rad, Mahdi Hasan Qommi

Our house was close to Ibrahim's. I was sixteen years old at that time and I would play volleyball with the youth in our neighbourhood every day. Other times, I would look after the pigeons on the roof. At that time, I had around one hundred and seventy pigeons. When the adhan was recited, my brother would go to the mosque, but I had never made a habit of attending the mosque.

One afternoon, Ibrahim was standing outside of his house on crutches, watching us play. During the game, the ball fell near Ibrahim and I went to get it. Ibrahim picked the ball up, spun it on his index finger and said, "Here, Agha Javad." I was shocked that he knew my name. Until the end of the game, I kept my eye on him, wondering how he knew my name.

A few days later, we were playing again. Ibrahim came and asked if he could play. I said, "If you want, do you even play volleyball?" He replied, "Well, if I don't know how to play, I'll learn from you!" He put his crutches on the side and started playing while limping. I have never seen somebody play as good as he did that time. He served the ball and returned it very well despite having to stand in one place due to his injury. That night, I said to my brother, "Do you know that Agha Ibrahim? He plays volleyball so well!" My brother laughed and said, "You still don't know him properly. Ibrahim was the high school volleyball champion. On top of that, he was also the wrestling champion." I exclaimed, "Are you being serious?! So why didn't he say anything?" He replied, "I don't know, but just know that he is a great man."

A few days later, Ibrahim came along while we were playing. Both sides wanted him on their team. We then started playing. He used to play so well. Near the end of the game, the sound of the adhan of Dhuhr came from the mosque. He held the ball and asked, "Guys, will you come with me to the mosque?" We said yes and went to pray in congregation.

A few days passed and we had fallen in love with Ibrahim. We would go to the mosque for him. One day, he invited us for lunch, and we had a long conversation. From then on, I would follow him wherever he went. If I wouldn't see him for one day, I would start to miss him and feel very upset. We even went to do *Varzesh-e Bastani* together once.

One night, we were sitting in the road towards the end of his recovery when he wanted to return to the warfront. He was talking to me about the thirteen and fourteen-year-old soldiers who took part in Operation Fath ol-Mobin. As he was talking, he said one sentence which summed up the whole conversation, "Even though they are younger and smaller than you, they managed to display great heroism with their trust in Allah, all while you are sitting here, looking up at the skies to see what your pigeons are doing!"

The next day, I released all my pigeons and set off for the warfront. Years have passed since that night. Now that I'm specialised in educational affairs, I understand how well Ibrahim managed to nurture us. He would do amr bil ma'ruf and nahy anil munkar[96] very smartly. He would act so brilliantly that he is a role model for those who claim to understand the art of nurturing, especially at a time when no one even spoke about the different methods of nurturing the youth.

It was the fifteenth of Shaban. As I turned onto my road with Ibrahim, we noticed that it was very beautifully decorated with lights. The youth of the neighbourhood were gathered at the end of the road. When we got closer, we realised that they were gambling with cards. When Ibrahim saw this, he got very angry but said nothing. I went up to the youth and introduced Ibrahim by

---

96   Encouraging people towards good and forbidding them from evil which is one of the obligations in Islam

saying, "He is one of my friends and he is a champion of volleyball and wrestling." All the youth came around and said salaam. He then gave me some money without anyone noticing and said, "Go buy ten ice-creams and come back quickly." That night, Ibrahim befriended the youth in our neighbourhood through ice-cream, conversation and laughter. In the end, he mentioned that gambling is haram. When we left the road, we saw all the cards ripped into pieces, floating in the gutter.

CORRECT CONDUCT
Narrator: Some of the martyr's friends

I was sitting behind Ibrahim on his motorcycle as we were riding down 17 Shahrivar Street. Suddenly, another motorcyclist quickly drove out of a side road onto the main street right in front of us. He turned towards us and Ibrahim had to brake so hard that he nearly fell off. The youth had a thug-like appearance and shouted, "Hey, what are you doing?!" He then stopped and looked at us angrily. Everybody knew he was the one at fault, and I wanted Ibrahim, who had a toned body, to get off and answer him properly. Instead, he smiled at the youth and replied to his rude behaviour by saying, "Salaam, how are you?" The angry motorcyclist was taken aback. He wasn't expecting an answer like that. He paused for a moment and then replied, "Salaam. Sorry, forgive me." He then went on his way and we went on ours. On the way, Ibrahim started answering all the questions I had in my mind. "Did you see what happened?" he said, "With one salaam, he calmed down. If I started to shout and fight instead, nothing would have been gained except for stress and breaking my morals."

Ibrahim's manner of doing amr bil maruf and nahy anil munkar was unique. If he wanted to tell somebody not to do something, he would try to say it indirectly. For example, he would talk about the bad effects of the act from a medical, social or another viewpoint so that they would reach the correct conclusion themselves. Only then would he bring evidence from the religious commands.

One of Ibrahim's friends lacked control over his eyes and was always thinking about immoral acts. A few of his other friends were unable to change his behaviour. They tried shouting at him, hitting him, and, eventually, keeping away from him but nothing worked. However, Ibrahim was very close to him. He even took him to the gym and would respect him in front of the others. A while later, Ibrahim talked to him. First, he made a sense of honour and dignity boil up from within him by saying, "What would you do if someone goes after your mother or sister and starts harassing them?" He replied angrily, "I'll rip his eyes out!" Ibrahim then said calmly, "Well, my friend, if you have this much honour and dignity when protecting your women, why do you do the same thing?" He added, "Look, if everyone starts chasing other people's women, then all of the society would be destroyed." Ibrahim then talked about why looking at *non-mahram*[97] women is haram in Islam and he told him about the Prophet (s)'s saying, "Lower your gaze so that you see wonders."[98] He then brought other reasons to back his point up and the youth accepted all of his explanations completely. Ibrahim then said, "Make your own decision, if you want to be my friend, you must stop doing these immoral acts!"

Ibrahim's correct conduct and strong reasoning triggered a

---

[97] A non-mahram woman is every woman who is not your mother, sister, aunt, niece, foster mother from whom you breastfed, a girl who had also breastfed from your foster mother, your mother-in-law and stepdaughter who was born to the woman you marry.

[98] Muntakhab Mizan al-Hikmah, vol. 10, pg. 72

complete change in the youth's behaviour. He became one of the good youths of the neighbourhood and put all his wrongdoings behind him. This youth is only one example of many of the people that Ibrahim changed through kind behaviour, well-timed conversation and strong reasoning. Now, one of the roads of our neighbourhood is named after this youth.[99]

It was autumn of 1982 and we were going towards Azadi Square. I was dropping Ibrahim off at the west terminal of the city so that he could return to the warfront. A fancy car passed by us and a woman was sitting next to the driver without a proper hijab on. She glanced at Ibrahim and abused him! Ibrahim told me to chase them. I chased them as fast as I could and eventually signalled to them to pull over. I thought to myself that there is going to be a fight today. The car pulled up on the side of the road and we did too. I was waiting to see how Ibrahim would act. He stayed on the motorcycle, said salaam and asked how the man was very politely. After seeing how we were dressed and recalling what his wife had done, the driver didn't expect such a warm greeting. After he replied to the salaam, Ibrahim began, "I must apologise, your wife has abused me and everybody who has a beard. I want to know that..." The driver interrupted and said, "I'm sorry, my wife made a mistake and both her and her words are stupid!" Ibrahim replied, "No Agha, don't speak like that. I just want to know if I took your wife's rights. Perhaps I did something improper for her to act this way with me?!" The driver didn't expect us to act like this at all. He got out of his car, kissed Ibrahim's face and said, "No, my dear friend, you didn't do anything wrong. We made a mistake and we are very embarrassed." After thoroughly apologising, he

---

[99] The culture in Iran is that whenever someone is martyred, the road in which they lived on is named after them.

went on his way.

This kind of behaviour from Ibrahim was very strange for us, especially during that era, but this taught us how to correctly interact with others. He would always say, "In life, the one who is patient and doesn't act illogically in the face of anger is always more successful." This was the secret of his interactions with others. The way he would interact with others reminded me of the following verse of the Qur'an:

"And the servants of Allah, the Beneficent, are those who walk on the earth with humility and when the ignorant talk to them, they say peace be upon you."[100]

THE TALE OF THE SNAKE

Narrator: Mahdi Amuzadeh

It was ten o'clock at night and we were playing football in the street. I had heard Agha Ibrahim's name from the youth in the neighbourhood, but I had never met him. As we were playing, I noticed somebody walking down the road on crutches. I recognised him by his long beard and wounded leg. He stood on the side of the road and watched us play. One of the youths asked him if he wanted to play, and he replied, "I can't play with this foot, but if you want, I can play in goal." I could play very well, but I wasn't able to score against him despite my best efforts. He was playing like a professional. About half an hour later, he stopped the ball with his foot and said, "Guys, don't you think it's a bit late now and people might want to sleep?" So, we gathered the goalposts and the ball and sat around him. One of the youths said, "If you can, please tell us some memories you have from the warfront." That night, I heard such strange stories that I am yet to forget. Agha Ibrahim narrated:

---

[100] Surah Furqan, verse 63

"I had gone on a reconnaissance operation with Javad Afrasyabi in the west of the country. It was midnight, and we were hiding near the Iraqi trenches. As the sun rose and we were completing our reports on the enemy positions, I suddenly saw a huge snake moving right towards our hiding place. I had never seen such a big snake in my life. I couldn't breathe out of fear. We couldn't do anything. If we shot the snake, the Iraqis would find us, and if we ran away, they would see us. The snake was moving towards us very quickly, so fast that we didn't have enough time to make a decision. I sat down, closed my eyes, said, 'In the name of Allah' and then asked Allah to help me by the right of Lady Fatimah (a). Those seconds passed like hours. A few moments later, Javad shook my arm and I opened my eyes. I was surprised to see that the snake had come very close to us and then changed direction, moving away from us."

That night, Ibrahim told us some funny stories as well and we laughed a lot. He then told us, "Try not to play in the middle of the night when people are resting."

From the next day onwards, I followed Ibrahim wherever he went. When I learnt that he would go to the mosque to pray Fajr, I would go to the mosque to see him. He had such an effect on me and the other children of the neighbourhood to the extent that we started to pray slowly and carefully as he would. A while later when he was left for the warfront, we couldn't bear to be separated from him and we also set off for the warfront.

THE PLEASURE OF ALLAH

Narrator: Abbas Hadi

One of Ibrahim's qualities was that nobody would find out about anything he had done other than those who were with him and saw him do it themselves. He wouldn't speak about what he had done unless it was completely necessary. He would always say, "Things that are done to attain the pleasure of Allah are not to be said," or, "The problem is that we work to please everyone except Allah."

Imam Ali (a) said, "Whoever clears his heart and actions from everything other than Allah, He will love him."[101] The great mystics emphasise the following point: something is only valuable if done in the way of Allah. On the other hand, every breath one takes in the cause of anything except Allah is to his loss in the Hereafter.

When Ibrahim was wounded, I went to one of the gyms in Tehran with him and sat in a corner. Whenever one of the more experienced members would enter, the head of the gym would ring the bell and the exercise would pause momentarily. The person who had just entered would wave at the other members and sit in the corner, smiling. Ibrahim was watching attentively. He then turned back and said to me softly,

"Look at how happy the sound of the bell makes them. Some people love the gym bell. If they loved Allah as much as the whistle, they wouldn't be standing on the ground, but rather, walking among the clouds. The world is like this; if people love the world and are attached to it, their everyday life is the same. However, if one raises his head to the skies and does everything for the pleasure of Allah, be assured that his life would change. At that point, he will realise the true meaning of living. In the gym, many want to see who is the strongest and who gets tired sooner. If you ever become the leader of the exercise, change the exercises frequently when you see somebody is becoming tired for the sake of Allah. When I was the leader of the exercise, I didn't do this. Of course, I didn't have any ulterior motives, but they still talked about me behind my back, so you don't do this!"

He would say, "A person must do everything for the pleasure of Allah, even his personal activities."

---

[101] Ghurar al-Hikam, p. 538

As the sun rose on Friday, Ibrahim returned with his clothes drenched in blood! He changed his clothes carefully [so that the impurity does not spread] and told me after praying, "Abbas, I'm going upstairs to sleep." Around noon, somebody started pounding on the door and wouldn't stop. Our mother went to open the door and saw that it was the woman who lived next door. After saying salaam, she snapped, "Is your Ibrahim the same age as my son?! Last night, he took my son out on his motorcycle, then they crashed, and my son's foot was fractured." She added, "Look, ma'am, I sent my son to the best high school. I don't want him spending time with people like your son." Our mother was completely unaware of what happened and became very upset. She apologised and exclaimed, "I don't know what you are talking about, but sure, I will talk to Ibrahim. Please forgive us." I was listening to the conversation, so I ran upstairs. I woke Ibrahim up and asked, "What did you do?!" Ibrahim asked, "Why? What happened?" I asked, "You crashed last night?!" He got up in shock and asked, "Crash?! What are you talking about?!" I replied, "Didn't you hear? Mohammad's mother was at the door and she was screaming." Ibrahim thought a little and answered, "Thank God, it's nothing serious."

That afternoon, Mohammad's mother and father came by to visit Ibrahim with a box of cakes and flowers. His mother was constantly apologising, and our mother asked in confusion, "There's a big difference between what you were saying this morning and now!" Mohammad's mother responded, "I swear to God, I don't know what to say, I'm so embarrassed. Mohammad told us everything that happened. He said he didn't know what would have happened had Ibrahim not arrived. The youth of the neighbourhood told me that he and Ibrahim were together and got into a crash to stop us from getting worried. I'm so disappointed that I judged your son like that, please forgive me. I have been saying to Mohammad's father that it is bad that Ibrahim has been injured for a few months and he still hasn't healed, yet we hadn't come to visit him." Our mother asked, "I don't understand, what happened to Mohammad?"

The lady said, "At midnight on Thursday night, the youth of the mosque committee were busy at the checkpoint. Mohammad was in the middle of the road with other volunteer soldiers. Suddenly, he accidentally pulled the trigger on his gun and shot himself in the leg. He fell in the street and started losing a lot of blood from his leg. At that moment, Agha Ibrahim arrived on his motorcycle. He ran to Mohammad and bandaged his leg with help from another of his friends, and then he took him to the hospital." Once the lady stopped speaking, I looked back at Ibrahim. He was sitting in the corner very peacefully; he knew well that someone who does something for the pleasure of Allah mustn't pay attention to what others say.

SINCERITY

Narrator: Abbas Hadi

I would talk to Ibrahim about exercise. He would say, "Whenever I would go to exercise or take part in a wrestling competition, I would always be in wudu. Every time I would go for a wrestling competition, I would pray a two-unit prayer." I asked him what kind of prayer he would pray, and he replied, "A *mustahabb* one! I would pray to Allah that I don't hurt anybody else's feelings during the tournament." Ibrahim would never even think of sinning, and for this reason, he was a role model for all his friends. Even if they would talk about sin, he would quickly change the subject. Whenever he saw that his friends were backbiting, he would constantly tell them to recite a Salawat, or he would change the subject however he could. He would never talk badly of anyone except if he wanted the person to correct his behaviour. He would never wear tight or short-sleeved clothes. He would always do the hardest jobs available, and when I asked him why he explained, "It is important for the nafs."

Shaheed Ja'far Jangravi narrated, "After the programme ended, we all sat with each other and started talking. Ibrahim was sitting alone in the other room, deep in thought. When everybody left, I went to Ibrahim. He still hadn't noticed that I'd entered the room. I saw that every few moments or so, he would scratch his face and behind his eyelid with a needle. I blurted out suddenly, "What are you doing, Agha Ibrahim?!" When he noticed me, he jumped. After a short pause, he replied, "Nothing, nothing, it was nothing!" I replied, "I swear by your life, you have to tell me why you were scratching your face with a needle!" He paused, and then said quietly like someone who had committed a crime, "This is the punishment of the eye that looks at a non-mahram." At that time, I didn't understand what he was doing or what he meant. However, when I read the biographies of the great people later, I read that they would reprimand themselves to prevent themselves from sinning."

Another of Ibrahim's outstanding characteristics was that he would keep away from non-mahram women. If he wanted to speak to a non-mahram woman, he would never raise his head under any circumstances, even if she was a relative. It got to a point that his friends would joke that Ibrahim had an allergy to non-mahram women! Imam Muhammad Baqir (a) put it so beautifully, "Talking to non-mahram women is one of Satan's arrows."

Ibrahim put great emphasis on feeding others. He would always invite his friends over for food. While he was injured, he enjoyed cooking and feeding the people who would visit him every day. He would tell his friends, "We are only a means [of Allah] and this is your sustenance. A believer's sustenance has blessings." He used to do the same for lectures and religious gatherings. When he saw that the host of the programme was unable to prepare food, he would make food for everybody there without saying a word. He would say, "Imam Husayn (a)'s mourning must be perfect from every aspect." He would make food for the revolutionary committee meeting on Thursday nights. After eating, we would go to do ziyarah of Shah Abdul-Azeem (a) or we would go to Behesht-e Zahra together.

The revolutionary religious youth will never forget that era even though it didn't last very long. I asked Ibrahim once, "Where do you get all this money from? You only earn two thousand tomans from the Education and Nurturing Department monthly, but you spend a lot more than that on others." He looked into my eyes and replied, "Allah gives sustenance and we are His means during these programmes. I prayed to Allah so that my pocket never be empty. Allah gives me money from places I cannot even think of."

THE PEOPLE'S NEEDS AND ALLAH'S BLESSINGS

Narrator: Some of the martyr's friends

I was with Ibrahim as we were returning from a relatively long journey by motorcycle. An old man was standing on the side of the street with his family. The man started waving at us and I stopped. He asked for directions and after we told him where he had to go, he started telling us about his difficulties. One wouldn't be able to guess from his appearance that he was an addict or a beggar. Ibrahim got off the bike and started searching his trouser pockets, but he had nothing on him. He asked, "Amir, do you have any money?" I searched my pockets, but I didn't have anything either. Ibrahim said, "Please look again, for God's sake!" I looked again but I had nothing on me. We apologised to that old man and we set off once again.

On the way, I looked in my wing mirror and I noticed that Ibrahim was crying. The weather wasn't so cold that it could cause tears, so for that reason, I stopped on the side and asked, "Ibrahim dear, are you crying?" He wiped his face and replied, "We were not able to help someone needy." I replied, "Well, we didn't have money, there's no sin in this." He replied, "I know, but I felt sorry for him and we were not blessed with being able to help him." I paused and didn't say anything. We then set off again, but I was secretly envious of Ibrahim. The next day, I saw Ibrahim. He was saying, "I will never leave home without money ever again so that we don't have a repetition of yesterday's events."

The way Ibrahim would help resolve other people's problems reminded me of Imam Husayn (a)'s saying, "Know that fulfilling people's needs is one of Allah's blessing upon you, so do not be burdened by fulfilling them such that they switch to someone other than you."[102]

Towards the end of Ibrahim's recovery, he called me and after saying salaam, he asked if I was using my car that day. I replied, "No, it's just sitting outside the house." He came, took the car and told me that he would return by the afternoon. He brought the car back in the afternoon, and I asked him, "Where did you want to go?" He replied, "Nowhere, I did some taxi driving for a bit." I replied, laughing, "Are you joking?!" He said, "No. Now, if you're not busy, come, let's go, I have a few things to do." As I was going inside the house, he added, "If you have things inside

---

[102] Bihar al-Anwar, vol. 78, pg. 121

that you don't use like rice and oil, bring those as well." I picked up some oil and rice and we went to a shop. Ibrahim bought some meat, chicken and other things and got back in. When he paid the shopkeeper, I noticed that he paid him in change, so I figured that must have been the money from the taxi driving.

We then went to the south of the city and visited a few houses I didn't recognise. Ibrahim would knock, give them the groceries and say, "We have come from the warfront, these are your rations." Ibrahim spoke in a certain way to not embarrass the people, and he was not boastful about it either.

I later learnt that those houses we visited belonged to families whose breadwinners had gone to the warfront, and for this reason, Ibrahim would take care of them. His behaviour reminded me of Imam Sadiq (a)'s saying, "Striving to help your fellow Muslims in their affairs is greater than doing tawaf[103] of the Ka'bah seventy times and ensures one's safety on the Day of Judgment."[104] This narration was the slogan of Ibrahim's life. He had dedicated his life to helping others.

When Ibrahim was in high school, he would work at the bazaar in the afternoons and had a steady income. He learnt that one of the neighbours had severe financial difficulties. They had no one to pay for their basic needs since their breadwinner had recently passed away. Whenever Ibrahim received his salary every month, he would secretly give that money to supply the family with their needs without telling anyone. Whenever there was extra food cooked in the house, he would always send it for them. He continued doing so for years until his martyrdom, and no one knew about this except his mother.

---

103   Going around the Ka'bah, which is a part of the Haj rituals
104   Bihar al-Anwar, vol. 74, pg. 318

Somebody had come asking for Ibrahim. He was previously a janitor but had recently lost his job. He came to ask for financial support. However, instead of giving him money, Ibrahim found a suitable job for him by referring to a few friends.

He would do anything to resolve others' difficulties, and if he couldn't do something, he would ask his friends and get them to help. However, he would always observe one rule: he mustn't encourage begging through his help. Ibrahim would always tell his friends, "Try to resolve someone's problem before he turns to you to beg." He would help any of his friends who were going through difficulties or anyone who he thought may have financial difficulties. He would do it secretly before the other party could say anything, and then he would say, "I don't need it for now. I'm giving this to you as a loan. Give it back to me whenever you can." He would never ask for the money back. When he would help others, he would take care of their reputations as well. He would always act in such a way that the other party wouldn't feel embarrassed.

The great religious personalities advise us that if we want to resolve our problems, we should strive to help others resolve theirs. They also say to feed others to the extent of one's capability and in this manner, many of our problems will be resolved.

Ibrahim came to our house as the sun was setting on one of the days of the month of Ramadan. He said salaam and asked how we were. He then borrowed a large pot from me and went to a traditional Iranian breakfast shop. I went with him and asked, "Ibrahim dear, opening your fast with breakfast?! That must be so nice!" He replied, "You're right, but it's not for me." He bought one portion and some bread, and as soon as we left the shop, Eeraj turned up on his motorcycle. Ibrahim got on and bade farewell to me. I thought to myself, "They've probably gathered a couple of friends and are opening their fasts together." I was so upset that they didn't even offer me any! The next day, I saw Eeraj and I asked, "Where did you guys go yesterday?" He replied, "There was a little home at the end of the road behind Chehel Tan Park. We knocked on the door and gave them the food. The old man and the children who came to the door were very grateful. They knew Ibrahim from before, and they were a very poor family. After that, I dropped Ibrahim off at his house."

Twenty-six years after Ibrahim's martyrdom, I saw in my dream that he had come to Tehran in a military vehicle. I was so happy; I didn't know what to do. His face was very radiant. I went forward and we hugged one another. I shouted out of joy, saying, "Guys, come, Agha Ibrahim has come back!" Ibrahim said, "Come, get in, we've got a lot to do." We set off together and stopped outside a tall building. The engineers and the owner of the building all came to say salaam to Agha Ibrahim. They all knew him well. Ibrahim turned to the owner and said, "I have come to give a good reference for this Sayyid. Reserve one of the flats for him," and then he pointed at someone standing a little further away from us. The owner said, "Agha Ibrahim, this man neither has the money nor is he able to get a loan. How am I meant to give him a flat?" I agreed with him and explained, "Ibrahim dear, those times have passed. People only recognise cash nowadays!" Ibrahim looked at me meaningfully and said, "I have only returned to resolve the problems of a few people like him. Otherwise, I have no business here!" He then went back to the car. As I was about to follow him, my mobile phone rang, and I woke up.

KHUMS

Narrator: Mostafa Saffar Harandi

One of the scholars Ibrahim loved dearly was the late Haj Agha Harandi. This great scholar would work as a cloth seller when it wasn't time for prayers.

Towards the end of the summer of 1982, I accompanied Ibrahim to Agha Harandi's shop. Ibrahim bought some cloth the size of two shirts. The next week, I saw that Ibrahim at the mosque at prayer time and he went to speak to Haj Agha. I went to see what was happening and realised that Ibrahim was busy calculating his khums[105]. I couldn't stop myself from laughing; he never kept anything for himself, he would always spend it on others, so what money did he want to give khums on?! Agha Harandi calculated the khums of the year and told him, "Your khums for this year is 400 tomans." He continued, "However, with the permission I have from the respected maraji'[106] and what I know about you, I excuse you from paying." Still, Ibrahim insisted on paying his religious dues and eventually paid his khums. Ibrahim's actions reminded me of Imam Sadiq (a)'s saying, "Whoever does not pay Allah's rights [like khums] will spend two times that amount in the way of falsehood."[107]

After prayers, we went to Agha Harandi's shop again. He said to Haj Agha, "I want two pieces of cloth like the ones you gave us last week, please." Haj Agha looked at him with surprise and said, "My son, you have just bought cloth from me. This cloth is from the government and I'm not allowed to sell it above a certain limit." Ibrahim didn't say anything, but as I knew what had happened, I explained, "Haj Agha, Agha Ibrahim has given away the two

---

105 Khums is giving one fifth of your savings in the way of Allah and is one of the obligations of Islam

106 In Shia Islam, we are obligated to follow someone who is an expert in the religion and has studied it completely, and we call them the maraji' (sin. marja)

107 Athar al-Sadiqeen, vol. 5, pg. 466

shirts. Some people at the gym wear short-sleeved shirts or don't have a lot of money. That's why Ibrahim gave the shirts to them." After listening to what I had to say carefully, Haj Agha turned to Ibrahim, looked meaningfully at him and said, "I will give you cloth this time, but you don't have the right to give it to anyone else. If anyone else needs it, send them here."

WE LOVE YOU

Narrator: Javad Majlisi

It was autumn 1982, and we set off for the military regions alongside Ibrahim once again. This time, Ibrahim's recitations about Lady Fatimah (a) were the talk of the town. Wherever we went, they would talk about him.

Many of the soldiers narrated stories about his heroics on the battlefield that couldn't have been achieved without the intercession of Lady Fatimah (a). We went to the province of Sumar, and whichever trench we went to, they would ask Ibrahim to recite about Lady Fatimah (a) for them.

That night, Ibrahim started reciting for one of the battalions, but his voice was hoarse as he was exhausted, and the gathering had gone on for a long time. After the programme, one or two of the youth came up to him, joked with him and copied his voice. After that, they said some things that made him upset. That night before sleeping, Ibrahim was very angry and said, "I'm not important, but they took Lady Fatimah (a)'s majlis as a joke, and for that reason, I will never recite again!" I constantly said to him, "Don't take their words to heart, Agha Ibrahim, just do what you do best," but he wouldn't listen. That night, we returned to the base and he made the same promise there that he will never recite again! I finally slept at one o'clock in the morning, battered and exhausted.

I felt someone shaking my arm a little before the adhan of

Fajr. I opened my eyes with difficulty, and I saw Ibrahim's radiant face looming over me. He called me and said, "Get up, it's time for adhan!" I got up and thought to myself, "It's as if he doesn't know what the meaning of fatigue is!" Of course, I knew that whatever time he would sleep, he would always manage to wake up an hour before the adhan, and he would start praying. He woke the others up and recited the adhan. We then all prayed Fajr in congregation. After praying and reading tasbih, Ibrahim started reciting supplications, and then, to my surprise, he recited for Lady Fatimah (a)! Ibrahim's beautiful poems made tears run down everyone's faces. I was more surprised than everyone else as I had heard him swear the night before that he would never recite ever again, but I didn't say anything.

After breakfast, we went back to the province of Sumar. On the way, I could only think about Ibrahim's strange actions. Ibrahim looked at me profoundly and asked, "You want to ask me why I recited this morning even though I swore I wouldn't?" I replied, "Well yes, you did say last night that..." He interrupted me, saying, "What I'm about to say to you, you have no right to share with anyone else as long as I am alive." He paused for a bit and continued, "Last night, I couldn't sleep, but around midnight, I dozed off for a bit. I dreamt that Lady Fatimah (a) had come and she said, 'Don't say that you won't recite, we love you. Whoever asks you to recite, recite for them!'" His tears didn't allow him to continue. From that day onwards, Ibrahim continued reciting.

OPERATION ZAYN AL-ABIDEEN (A)

Narrator: Javad Majlisi

It was December 1982. Normally, wherever Ibrahim would go, he would be met with open arms. Many of the commanders had heard

of Ibrahim's bravery and courage. He also came to our battalion one time and we spoke to each other for a while. Eventually, my battalion was ready to leave. When I came back, our commander asked me where I had been and I replied, "One of my friends visited me. He is now leaving in a car." He looked back and asked who my friend was, so I told him it was Ibrahim Hadi. He looked at me with surprise and asked, "Is that the Ibrahim that everyone is talking about?" and I told him it was. He asked me while watching the car drive away, "He's one of the war veterans, how did he become friends with you?" I said proudly, "Well, he is from our neighbourhood in Tehran." He turned back and said to me, "Bring him here one day so that he can talk with the soldiers." I replied, "He is a very busy man, but we'll see what happens."

The next day, I went to the Operations Headquarters to see Ibrahim. After exchanging pleasantries and talking for a bit, he said, "Wait, let me drop you off and speak to your commander." We then set off for my battalion's base in a Toyota. On the way to the base, we reached a waterway which we would get stuck in whenever we would try to cross it, so I said, "Agha Ibrahim, cross from up there, you'll get stuck here." He said, "I don't have time, we'll cross from here." I said, "You don't need to come anyway, thank you for bringing me here but I will make the rest of the way myself." He replied, "Sit down. I want to see your commander," and he started driving. I thought to myself, "How does he expect to drive through all of this water?" I laughed to myself and thought, "It will be hilarious if he gets stuck! Maybe he'll finally learn a lesson!" Somehow though, Ibrahim said one 'Allahu Akbar' and 'Bismillah' loudly and managed to cross the water in first gear! When we reached the other side, he said, "We still don't understand the power of 'Allahu Akbar'. If we did know it, most of our problems would be solved."

Our battalion was fully prepared for the new operation, and a few days later, we were ready to advance towards Sumar. I went and waited at the three-way junction as Ibrahim told me that he would come before sunset. My battalion left but I was impatiently looking out towards the desert road until I saw Ibrahim's beautiful face from afar. He would normally come without a weapon and wearing Kurdish trousers, but this time, unlike normal, he came wearing camouflage clothes, a headband and was carrying an AK-47. I went forward and asked, "Ibrahim, how come you're carrying a weapon?" He laughed and replied, "Obeying the commander is obligatory. I came like this because my commander ordered me to." I asked him, "Agha Ibrahim, will you let me come with you?" and he replied, "No, stay with your group. We are right behind you, so we will see each other."

We walked for a few kilometres, and eventually, we reached enemy lines under the cover of darkness. I was the RPG firer. Hence, I was ahead of the rest, walking with the commander of the battalion. Everything seemed wrong and I didn't feel right at all. The province was too quiet! We were moving towards the top of a hill through a narrow valley with a slight slant. We could see the Iraqi trenches at the top of the hill, and I was commanded to destroy them once we reached them. I looked around the hill and I saw that trenches had been made on both sides at the bottom and along to the top of the hill. The Iraqis knew that we were going to come through this valley! I gritted my teeth and walked in such a way to not make a sound, and the rest copied me. I was so afraid; I didn't dare to even breathe! As we were about to reach the top of the hill, a flare was fired, and the sky lit up. At that moment, missiles and bullets started to rain down upon us from all three sides. We all laid down on the ground. We were directly within the enemy's shooting range. Every second, a grenade was thrown, or a bullet was fired towards us, and the injured were crying out in pain. We couldn't do anything in that darkness. I wanted the earth to open and swallow me. I could saw death right in front of my eyes. While I was in this state, someone came crawling and grabbed my foot. I lifted my head to look back and couldn't believe my eyes. It was Ibrahim! He exclaimed, "Oh, it's you?!" He then took the RPG from me and went forward. He fired the RPG with the call of 'Allahu Akbar' and the trench in front of us which was firing the most blew up. He got up and called out, "Oh Shias of Amir al-Mu'mineen (a), get up, the hand of our master is with us [i.e. the Imam is helping us]!" This raised the soldiers' spirits. I also shouted 'Allahu Akbar' as the rest got up, and everyone started shooting. Almost all the Iraqis fled, and a few moments later, I saw Ibrahim standing at the top of the hill! It didn't take too long to then liberate the key hill of the Iraqis. Some enemy forces were taken as prisoners, and the rest of the soldiers continued forward. I went forward with the commander, and he said to me on the way, "Now I can see why everybody wants to be with Ibrahim in the operations; he is so fearless!"

Around midnight, I saw Ibrahim again and he stated, "Did you see how our master helped us? We only shouted 'Allahu Akbar' once and the enemy fled!"

The operation in our area ended so all the soldiers in the battalions went back on leave. However, some of the battalions left their wounded and martyred soldiers behind. Ibrahim was irate while speaking to one of the commanders. I had never seen him angry before then. He was shouting, "You had both provisions and manpower when you wanted to leave, so why didn't you look after the soldiers of your battalion?! Why did you leave the wounded behind?! Why?!" He planned with the commander of our area who was one of his friends, and he infiltrated enemy territory with Javad Afrasyabi and a few others. Over a few nights, they found several wounded and martyred soldiers who were left behind and sent them back. Due to the sensitivity of the area, the enemy was not able to clear that territory completely.

By the 12th of December 1982, Ibrahim and Javad were able to bring back eighteen wounded soldiers and nine martyrs from behind enemy lines. They even managed to skilfully bring a martyr back who had been martyred only ten metres away from the Iraqi trenches. After this operation, Ibrahim fell slightly ill, so we went back to Tehran together. He was in Tehran for a few weeks where he continued his cultural and religious activities.

THE LAST DAYS

Narrators: Ali Sadeghi, Ali Moqaddam

I returned to Tehran with Ibrahim in the middle of December. He was exuberant albeit exhausted. He would say, "No martyr or wounded soldier was left behind in the enemy's territory. We brought back whoever was there." He said, "Tonight, we have brought joy to many waiting eyes, and whenever one of these mothers of these martyrs visits the grave of her son, we will also receive a reward from Allah." I seized the opportunity and asked him, "Agha Ibrahim, so why do you pray that your body is lost at war?" He was not expecting such a question. He paused for a moment and replied, "I have prepared my mother, I have told her not to wait for me. I have even told her to pray for me to be lost at war," but once again, he didn't give me the answer I was looking for. I stayed in Tehran with Ibrahim for a few weeks. After he recovered from his illness and the fatigue of the operation, the youth would come to visit him every night. Wherever Ibrahim went, he would be surrounded by religious and revolutionary youth.

Towards the end of December, Ibrahim's personality began to change. He wouldn't joke as much, and most of the youth would call him 'Shaykh Ibrahim'. He trimmed his beard, but his face was still just as luminous as before. All the youth wanted to be martyred, but martyrdom meant something else to Ibrahim.

We were walking together at night, and I asked, "Your wish is martyrdom, right?" He laughed and replied after a few seconds of silence, "Martyrdom is but an iota of my wishes. I want nothing to remain of me. I want to be cut into pieces like my master Husayn (a) who had no shroud. I don't want my body to come back. I want to remain lost!" I already knew the reasoning behind his words. He would say, "I don't want to have a tomb as the mother of the Imams[108] had no tomb." After that, we went to the gym and he invited all the youth to his house for lunch on the following day.

At noon the next day, we went to his house. We all prayed in congregation before lunch. We made Ibrahim the Imam of the congregation. There was a strange aura around him during his prayers. It was as if he was not in this world but rather in the world of the angels! After prayers, he read *Dua Faraj*[109] beautifully. One of our friends turned around and said to me, "Ibrahim's behaviour has changed. I have never seen him cry like this during his prayers before."

During our programmes, Ibrahim would seek intercession from Lady Fatimah (a). He would add towards the end, "This is dedicated to all of the martyrs whose bodies are lost at war and

---

108 Lady Fatimah (a) was the mother of all the Imams except Imam Ali (a), her husband

109 Dua Faraj is a small supplication which is generally either recited during prayer in *qunut* or after prayers in which one seeks the hastening of the reappearance of Imam Mahdi (aj).

don't have a grave like the mother of the Imams." He would always mention the warfront and its soldiers during his recitations.

It was nine o'clock at night towards the end of January. Someone shouted from the road, "Haj Ali, are you home?" I went to the window and I saw Ibrahim and Ali Nasrollah on a motorcycle in the middle of the road. I was overjoyed and went to the door. I hugged Ibrahim and then Ali and brought them inside. It was very cold outside. I was home alone. I asked them if they had eaten dinner and Ibrahim replied, "No, don't worry about it." I said, "Stop being polite, let me make you some eggs." I then went and made a small dinner. I said, "My kids aren't here tonight. If you don't have anything to do, stay here, we have a free bed." Ibrahim accepted my invitation. I then said while laughing, "Ibrahim, you're still going around in Kurdish trousers in this cold weather! Do you not get cold?" He laughed and replied, "No, but after all, I am wearing four pairs of them!" He then took off three pairs of trousers and went to bed. I then continued talking with Ali.

I don't know whether Ibrahim had fallen asleep or not, but suddenly he jumped up, looked at me in the eyes and asked, "Haj Ali, be honest! Do I look ready for martyrdom?" I didn't expect him to ask me such a question. I looked at Ibrahim's face for a few moments and told him, "Some of the soldiers had a strange aura around them before their martyrdom, but to tell you the truth, Ibrahim dear, you are the same!" Silence descended upon the room. Ibrahim got up and said to Ali, "Get up, we have to go now." I exclaimed, "Ibrahim, where to?" He replied, "We have to go to the mosque quickly." He then put on his trousers and left with Ali.

FAKKEH, THE LAST STOP

Narrator: Ali Nasrollah

We reached the mosque at midnight. Ibrahim said goodbye to everyone and then he went home to say goodbye to his family. He asked his mother to pray that he is martyred. We left for the warfront in the early morning. Ibrahim was speaking less than normal and was reading the Qur'an and doing dhikr.

We got to the military encampment in North Fakkeh. The battalions were busy sorting out their strategies for the upcoming operation. The soldiers were all overjoyed when they heard that Ibrahim had returned. His tent was filled with the revolutionary youth. Haj Hosein [Allah-Karam] also came and was delighted to see Ibrahim. After exchanging pleasantries, Ibrahim asked, "Haj Hosein, all of the soldiers are busy. Is something happening?" He replied, "We are advancing for an operation tomorrow and we would be glad if you came with us." He then added, "I have to divide the scouts amongst the battalions. Every battalion must have one or two heads of reconnaissance." He then put a list in front of Ibrahim and asked, "What do you think of these soldiers?" Ibrahim read the list and gave his opinion on each one. He then asked, "Well Haji, how have the troops been divided now?" He responded, "Right now, the forces have been divided into four corps, and a corps comprises of several divisions. Haj Hemmat has been appointed the commander of the 11th Qadr Corps. The 27th Division is part of this corps. We are the reconnaissance heads of the 11th Qadr Corps."

That afternoon, Ibrahim dyed his beard with henna, trimmed his hair and groomed his beard. His beautiful face had become even more heavenly. In the evening, we went to one of the watchtowers in the area. He was examining the area in which the operation was to take place with a special pair of binoculars and was jotting a few things down on a piece of paper. Some of the other soldiers came to the watchtower and kept telling Ibrahim to hurry up and insisting that they wanted to see as well. Ibrahim couldn't control his anger and yelled, "Does this look like a cinema?! We have to prepare our strategies for tomorrow and understand our route!" He then stormed out. Later, he told me, "I'm feeling very anxious!" I comforted him, saying, "It's nothing to worry about, calm down!"

We went to one of the commanders of the Qadr Corps and Ibrahim said, "Haji, the ground in this province is strange. The terrain is soft and sandy, which means the soldiers won't be able to move freely. In addition to this, the Iraqis have set down a lot of dangerous obstacles. In your opinion, do you think we will be successful in this operation?" The commander replied, "Ibrahim dear, this is an order from head command. As the Imam said, 'We are to do our duty, the result is with Allah.'"

The next afternoon, the soldiers of the battalions were ready. The last eleven battalions from the 27th Hazrat-e Rasool (s) Division took their rations, and everyone was ready to move towards Fakkeh. I saw Ibrahim from afar, and when I looked at his face, I felt shivers go down my spine. His face had become even more heavenly and it was more radiant than ever. He was wearing an Arab scarf and a delightful overcoat. He came towards us and shook everyone's hands. I pulled him aside and exclaimed, "Ibrahim, your face is so luminous!" He took a deep breath and said regretfully, "The day Beheshti (ra) was martyred, I was very upset, but I thought to myself, 'Good for him that he went as a martyr, it would have been a shame had he died naturally.' Asghar Vesali, Ali

Qorbani, Qasim Tashakkori and many other friends of mine were all martyred, such that I now have more friends in Behesht-e Zahra than in Tehran." He paused a little and then continued, "There it is, Khorramshahr liberated, and I'm fearful lest the war ends, and I miss the opportunity of martyrdom. However, my trust is in Allah." He sighed and continued, "I want to be martyred, but I want the most beautiful kind of martyrdom." I was looking at him with wonder and I was waiting for him to continue. He added, tears forming in the corners of his eyes, "When no one can find you, no one recognises you, it's just you and our master and he sits above your head and lays your head in your lap; this is the most beautiful martyrdom!" I said, "Ibrahim, I beg you, please don't speak like that!" I then changed the subject and said, "It will be better if we move with the commanders so that they can help us whenever we need them to." He replied, "No, I want to be with the baseejis." We then moved towards the shock troops which were busy organising their troops. I asked, "Ibrahim, what provisions shall I bring for you?" He replied, "Only two grenades. If I need a weapon, I'll take one off the Iraqis."

Haj Hosein Allah-Karam was staring at Ibrahim from a distance. We went towards him and it was as though he couldn't peel his eyes off Ibrahim's face. He immediately hugged Ibrahim and they stayed like that for a few moments, as if they knew that this was to be their final meeting. Ibrahim then unfastened his watch and said, "Hosein, this is something to remember me by." Haj Hosein replied, his eyes damp with tears, "No Ibrahim dear, keep it for yourself, you will need it!" Ibrahim replied calmly, "No, I don't need it!" Haj Hosein was extremely overwhelmed and changed the topic. He said, "Ibrahim dear, there are two routes for the operation. The baseejis are going through the first one, and I am going through the second one with a few of the commanders and scouts. Come with us." Ibrahim replied, "I will go through the first route with the baseejis. Is that a problem?" Haj Hosein replied,

"No, however you feel comfortable." Ibrahim separated himself from his final material attachments. He then went to the battalions which were the shock troops for the operation and sat beside them.

OPERATION BEFORE THE DAWN

Narrator: Ali Nasrollah

The Kumayl Battalion were the shock troops of the southern area and were stationed near the bases. One of the division commanders came and addressed the soldiers:

"Brothers, tonight we are going to Fakkeh to start Operation Dawn[110]. The enemy has dug three huge trenches in your path which are parallel to the border to hinder your advances. They have also set down a few other dangerous obstacles, but Insha'Allah, after you pass these dangerous obstacles and the trenches, the operation will begin. Once you reach the bases at the borders of Tawusiyyah and Rushaydiyyah, the first stage of the operation will be complete. After that, fresh troops from the Sayyid ash-Shuhada (a) Division and the other soldiers will pass by you. In continuation of the operation, they will advance to the Iraqi city of al-Ammarah, and Insha'Allah, you will be successful in this operation." He mentioned the dangerous obstacles and the route for the operation, saying, "The route for the operation is narrow and runs through minefields, but Insha'Allah, you will achieve your goals which have been assigned to you earlier."

When he finished his speech, Ibrahim started reciting immediately in a way I had never heard him recite before. He was mourning and reciting as if he himself was oppressed. He started describing the calamities that befell Lady Zaynab (a), beat his chest and recited a beautiful couplet that I was hearing for the first time:

---

110 عمليات والفجر

"[Seek] peace in Zaynab's heart,
Look at how her heart has turned to blood!"

The soldiers were all beating their chests in reply to his recitation. He then started reciting about Lady Zaynab (a)'s captivity and the martyrs of Karbala. In the end, he said, "Tonight, you will either meet your Lord or you will be taken as a prisoner and you will bear their torture heroically like the aunt of the Imams."[111,112] After his heartrending and spiritual recitation, the soldiers all arose, their faces wet with tears. We prayed Maghrib and Isha. Since I had returned to the warfront with Ibrahim, I had been following him like a shadow and didn't leave his side for even a second. I picked up one of the heavy, portable bridges with Ibrahim, and we advanced with the troops.

Advancing on the sandy terrain of Fakkeh was torturous, especially with equipment weighing more than twenty kilos that each soldier had to carry. As well as the equipment, we were also carrying a heavy bridge in the same manner a coffin is carried. We were advancing in single file through a route plotted through the minefields. After walking for approximately twelve kilometres, we reached the first trench in the south of Fakkeh. The soldiers were too exhausted to move any further.

It was half-past nine on Sunday, the 6th of February. We crossed the trench with our portable bridges and ladders. A strange silence had descended upon the area, and the Iraqis hadn't fired even a single bullet. About fifteen minutes later, we reached the second trench and we crossed it too. We informed the head command of our progress via radio. A few minutes later, we reached the third trench. Ibrahim was still helping the soldiers near the second trench. He was making sure that the soldiers got over safely as there were different types of mines and dangerous

---

111   Lady Zaynab

112   It is strange as nearly all of those who Ibrahim recited for that night were either martyred or taken prisoner

obstacles scattered around the trench. As we had reached the third trench, this should have meant that we close to the border bases and that the next stage of the mission was to begin, but the commander of the battalion stopped the soldiers and exclaimed, "According to the map, we were meant to walk further, but it's very strange; we've arrived quicker than expected and there is no sign of the bases either!"

Almost all the soldiers had passed the second trench when suddenly, the sky of Fakkeh lit up as if it were daytime! It was as if the enemy had been anticipating our arrival with all their firepower. They were shooting at us with everything they had, from machine guns to mortars and artillery guns. The soldiers couldn't do anything as the barbed wire and minefields ahead of them were preventing them from advancing. A few of the soldiers jumped into the third trench while many others were finding it difficult to navigate the sandy terrain. Everyone was running here and there. Some of the soldiers climbed through the barbed wire and tried to take cover in the field, but they were martyred by the mines. The area was riddled with mines. Ibrahim knew this, so he ran towards the third trench and was shouting out to the soldiers not to stray from the path. Everyone was lying on the ground. There was nothing that we could do. The Iraqi fire support base knew which route we were going through and bombarded it precisely. The situation had become chaotic and everyone was running in a different direction. The only place that offered a little safety was the trenches.

I had lost Ibrahim in the darkness. I advanced until the third trench, but it was impossible to find anyone. I saw one of my friends and asked him if he had seen Ibrahim. He replied, "He walked past here a few minutes ago." As I was walking to and fro, I saw one of the commanders. He recognised me and said, "Go back to the route quickly and tell the troops who are on their way to go back. This trench neither offers space nor safety. Go and come back quickly." I followed the commander's orders and sent all the soldiers who were around the second trench and on their way forward back to our bases. We were also able to help a few wounded soldiers and bring them back. This duty took around two to three hours. I wanted to go back, but the other soldiers told me, "You can't go back!" I asked why, and they explained, "We have been ordered to fall back. There's no point in you going back because the reinforcements will be arriving in the morning."

I prayed Fajr an hour later. The sun was slowly rising, and I felt tired and hopeless. I asked whoever returned if they knew anything about Ibrahim but to no avail. A few minutes later, I saw Mujtaba. He was returning from the front line, exhausted and dusty. I asked him hopelessly, "Mujtaba, have you seen Ibrahim?" He said while walking towards me, "We were together about an hour ago." I jumped from my place with happiness and asked while walking towards him, "Well, where is he now?" He replied, "I don't know. I told him that we've been ordered to fall back, I said that we have a chance to return as long as it's dark, but we won't be able to do anything once the sun rises, but Ibrahim told me, 'The soldiers are in the trenches. I'm going to them and we will all come back together.'" Mujtaba continued, "Whilst I was talking to Ibrahim, a battalion from the Ashura Division came to us. Ibrahim quickly spoke with their commander and informed them of the order to fall back, and he sent me with them because I knew the way back. He took an RPG and a few rockets from them and went towards the trench. I don't know what happened to Ibrahim after that."

An hour later, I saw Meysam Lateefi coming back to our bases with a few wounded soldiers. I went to help him, and then I asked about what was going on. He replied, "These few wounded soldiers and I had fallen past the trenches among the hills when Ibrahim Hadi came to our rescue." I stopped in my tracks suddenly and exclaimed, "Ibrahim?! Well, what happened then?" He replied, "He gathered us with difficulty, and he brought us back by dawn.

On the way, we reached a trench which had some kind of sludge at the bottom of it. It was also quite wide. Ibrahim brought two stretchers and made a makeshift bridge from them. He took us over but he advanced."

Around ten o'clock in the morning, the army base in Fakkeh was full of commanders, and many were saying that a few battalions had been besieged by the enemy!

THE KUMAYL TRENCH
Narrator: Ali Nasrollah

I asked one of the heads of intelligence, "What do you mean that battalions have been besieged? Iraq hasn't pushed forward, and our soldiers are in the second and third trench." The officer replied, "From what we learnt from our reconnaissance, the third trench differs from the others. Iraq dug this trench and a few other smaller trenches in these past two to three days. These trenches are exactly parallel to the border but are smaller and filled with dangerous obstacles." He continued, "The shock troop battalions jumped into the trench so that they wouldn't be hit and once the sun rose, the Iraqi tanks came forward and closed off both sides of the trench. They've now started to bombard the trench." He paused for a few moments then added, "The Iraqis had created sixteen kinds of dangerous obstacles in the soldiers' route, and they went four kilometres deep! Also, the traitors had given complete information about the operation to the Iraqis." I was devastated. I inquired, "What shall we do now?" He answered, "If the soldiers can resist, we will launch the second stage of the operation and bring them back." At that moment, the radioman of the base announced, "News from the besieged battalions!" Everyone went quiet and the radioman continued, "It says that Brother Sabet-Niya has shaken hands with Brother Afshordi!" This short piece of news meant that the commander of the Kumayl Battalion had been martyred.

That afternoon, we received news that Haj Hoseini, the vice-commander of the Kumayl Battalion, had also been martyred, and Bankdar, the other vice-commander, had been severely wounded. All the soldiers in the base were distraught.

On the 9th of February, the soldiers were ready to launch a new attack on the province of Fakkeh. I saw one of my friends coming from the base and asked him what was going on. He replied, "The radioman of the Kumayl Battalion just called and said to Haj Hemmat, "The radio's battery is dying. Many of the soldiers have been martyred, pray for us. Send our salaam to the Imam and tell him that we will stand until our last breath." I asked, my heart broken, "What is our duty now? What should we do now?" He replied, "Trust in Allah. Go and get ready. The next stage of the operation will begin tonight."

At sunset, our artillery guns began to fire at the enemy's trenches with brilliant accuracy. The Hanzaleh Battalion and the other battalions started advancing until they reached close to the Kumayl Trench. They even managed to evade the dangerous obstacles and reach the third trench but due to the number of Iraqi soldiers, only a few of the soldiers who were besieged were able to leave the trench under the cover of darkness and come back. This attack was unsuccessful, and we returned to our trenches before sunrise. However, most of the soldiers of the Hanzaleh Battalion stayed in the trenches close to the border. In this attack, we managed to destroy much of the enemy's armoured equipment because of the soldiers' calculated fire.

On the 10th of February 1983, we could still hear scattered gunfire from inside the trench. We realised from this that the soldiers must still have been resisting. What we couldn't understand was how they could still have the resources to resist after four days of besiegement?!

At sunset, it was announced that the operation had come to an end and the rest of the troops went back on leave. I saw one of the soldiers who had returned from the trench the night before. He was saying, "You don't know what kind of a situation we were in. There was no food or water, our ammunition was running low, and the walls of the trench were riddled with different kinds of mines! Every few minutes, we would fire a few bullets to let them know that we were still alive, and the Iraqis would constantly announce on their loudspeakers for us to surrender."

That evening, the sun set as I held great sorrow in my heart. I went to higher ground and looked out with my binoculars. I could still see scattered explosions around the trench. My best friend Ibrahim was in that trench and there was nothing I could do to help him! That night, I rested a little and I returned to the front line on the next day.

The Iraqis were very sensitive towards the date of the 11th of February/22nd of Bahman (the anniversary of the Islamic Revolution), so they laid heavy fire on the trench. Our soldiers had cleared from the closest trenches to the front line, and everyone had come back to the base. I thought to myself, "Perhaps the Iraqis want to advance," but it was highly unlikely as the dangerous obstacles that they had set for us had prevented them from advancing as well.

In the afternoon, the amount of gunfire decreased so I took my binoculars out and went to a place where I could get a better view of the trench. I couldn't believe my eyes; thick smoke was emanating from the trench and I was constantly hearing the sound of explosions. I ran to the intelligence officers and cried out, "The Iraqis are finishing off the trench!" They watched on with their binoculars, but we could only see fire and smoke. However, I still had hope. I thought to myself, "Ibrahim has survived harsher conditions than this," but when I remembered what he said before the operation, I felt shivers run down my spine.

THE BLOODY SUNSET
Narrator: Ali Nasrollah

The afternoon of the 11th of February 1983 was the most painful time of those five days. The intelligence officers had gone to their trench. I looked with the binoculars again and close to sunset, I noticed something moving from afar. When I looked closer, I realised three people were running towards us. They were constantly falling and getting back up on the way. They were injured and tired, and it was clear that they must have come from the trench. I called the others and we went to higher ground. I ordered the soldiers to hold their fire. The three people reached our trenches as the sun had just set. As soon as they reached us, I ran up to them and asked them where they were coming from, but they were unable to speak due to sheer exhaustion. One asked for water, so I gave him a flask immediately. The other was shivering from extreme hunger and weakness. The third one was drenched in blood.

When they recovered, they informed me that they were from the Kumayl Battalion. I asked agitatedly, "What happened to the other soldiers?" He stated, lifting his head with great difficulty, "I don't think there anyone else survived except us." I was feeling restless and asked them, "How did you manage to resist for these five days?!" He was too tired to speak. He paused for a few moments to swallow his food and answered, "We were hiding amongst the bodies for the past two days, but there was one person who kept us on our toes." He caught his breath and continued calmly, "What a man he was! He would fire an RPG in one direction and a machine gun in the other. He was so strong!" The other interrupted him and added, "He laid the bodies of the martyrs side by side at the end of the trench. He would ration the food and water, look after the wounded; it was as if this boy didn't understand the meaning of exhaustion!" I asked, "Weren't all of the commanders and vice-commanders of your battalion martyred? So, who are you talking about?!" He replied, "He was a youth I didn't know. He had short hair and he was wearing Kurdish trousers." The other chimed in, "He was wearing an Arab scarf around his neck on the first day. He had such a beautiful voice. He would recite for us and raise our spirits." My head felt light and I took a deep breath; they were describing Ibrahim! I sat down worriedly, held his hands and pleaded, "You're talking about Ibrahim, right? Where is he now?" He replied, "Yeah, I think so. One or two of the older soldiers would call him Agha Ibrahim." I yelled out, "Where is he now?!" One of the others replied, "He was alive until the last moments of the Iraqi bombardment. He then said to us, 'The Iraqis have moved their troops back, so they must want to wage a heavy attack. If you have the energy to, while this place is empty of Iraqi troops, retreat.' He then went and tended to the injured and we retreated." The other said, "I saw that they hit him, and he fell to the floor after one of the first explosions." I felt my body go weak and tears started rolling down my face. I couldn't control myself anymore. I put my face in the dust and wept. I recalled all the memories I had shared with him, from the ring of the gym to Gilan-e Gharb to other places.

The intense smell of gunpowder coupled with the sound of the explosions. I went to the edge of our trenches to go to the trench. One of the soldiers stood in my way and asked, "What are you doing? If you go, it won't bring Ibrahim back. Just look at how they're bombarding the trench!"

That night, they sent everybody in Fakkeh back on leave. All the other soldiers were in the same state as I was. Many had left their friends behind. As we entered the Dokouheh Province, Haj Sadiq Ahangaran was reciting on the radio, "Oh those returning from their journey, where are your martyrs, where are your martyrs?" The soldiers all started to weep even more.

The news of Ibrahim's martyrdom and being lost at war spread through the troops like wildfire. One of the soldiers who had come to the warfront with his son came to me and said woefully, "We are all mourning for Ibrahim. I swear to God that even if my son was martyred, I wouldn't be this upset. No one knows what a great man Ibrahim was."

The next day, they sent all the soldiers on leave and we returned to Tehran. No one dared to announce the news of Ibrahim's martyrdom, but a few days later, the news of him being lost at war had spread to everyone.

THE PEAK OF OPPRESSION

Narrator: Mahdi Ramazani

Despite my tender age, Allah gave me the blessing of accompanying His greatest servants in the Kumayl Battalion. On the night of the operation launch, we reached the third trench. This trench was small and was around a metre deep. On the contrary, the second trench was large and full of dangerous obstacles. That night, all the soldiers returned to the second trench, a trench which was later dubbed the Kumayl Trench. I spent five days in this trench with the other troops.

From the next morning, the Iraqi snipers would target anything that moved. During those days of besiegement, there was a very wonderful atmosphere in the trench. I remember that Ibrahim Hadi would keep us on our toes with his physical strength and courage. The commander and vice-commanders of

our battalion had all been martyred or wounded. For this reason, Ibrahim was the only person who kept us organised. He would divide the troops such that every three people would form a group and he stationed each group in the trench at a determined distance from the other. A person was standing on the edge of the trench, assessing the situation and two others were standing beside him inside the trench.

At the end of the trench, there was a curve. Ibrahim and a few others would move the martyrs there so that soldiers wouldn't have to see their martyred friends. He also laid the wounded in a corner so that they wouldn't be hurt. During those days, Ibrahim would recite the adhan and arrange the troops for prayers. Under those difficult circumstances, we would pray congregational prayers three times a day. Ibrahim would elevate the spirits of the soldiers by doing these things and made us hopeful of the future.

Two days after the launch of the operation and after the failed second stage of the operation, the soldiers increased their efforts to find a way out. In our last phone call with the army, Shaheed Commander Hajipour said sorrowfully, "There is nothing we can do. Try to return however you can."

On Thursday the 10th of February, we could hear more tanks and APCs from behind and in front of us. The soldiers had dug at the sides of the trenches and created a makeshift staircase. Some thought that reinforcements had come for us, but no, they had tightened the siege on us! The Iraqi commandos came out from among the tanks. They had realised that in the whole plain, there were only soldiers stationed in this trench. I remember a teenager by the name of Shaheed Sayyid Ja'far Taheri picked up an RPG, went up the stairs and destroyed an Iraqi tank with one accurate shot. This caused them to fall back a little. The soldiers killed a few of the commandos with their relentless fire and they took a few of the soldiers who had advanced a little too close to us as captives. In these difficult conditions, five Iraqi prisoners had now been added to our numbers. The lack of food and water had exhausted us. Most of the troops had fallen here and there in the trench, fatigued.

The tanks, which were a decent distance away from our trench, turned on their loudspeakers and one of the Iranian hypocrites announced, "Iranians, come and surrender. We have nothing to do with you. Cold water and food are awaiting you, come!" They would encourage us to surrender in this manner. Hunger and thirst had exhausted everyone to the extent that some of the soldiers said, "Come, let's surrender. We've done our duty, there is no hope for us to be rescued anymore." One of the baseeji teenagers said, "If we surrender and Iraqi television shows us off, and the Imam sees us and becomes upset, what will we do? Didn't we come to bring peace to the heart of the Imam?" After hearing these words, any thought of surrender was abandoned. When Ibrahim learnt of their decision, he was pleased and said, "So we must gather all the ammunition and food that we have and divide it amongst the soldiers." We gave whatever food or water we had left to Ibrahim. He gave every five soldiers a bit of food and one flask of water but gave each of the five Iraqi prisoners an individual flask. Some of the soldiers were upset about this but Ibrahim replied, "They are our guests!" We also gathered the ammunition and gave it to the soldiers who weren't wounded so that they could stand guard.

By the dawn of the next day, i.e. 11th of February, the Iraqi tanks moved back a little. Some of the troops took advantage of this opportunity and retreated in groups, but unfortunately, some of them triggered mines and were martyred. An hour later, the enemies started bombarding us with gunfire and missiles; there was nothing we could do.

In the afternoon, the enemy commandos finally managed to reach us after the heavy bombardment of the trench. Suddenly, we realised that the Iraqis had pointed their artillery guns toward us from above the trench. An Iraqi officer came into the trench using the stairs the soldiers had created, and another soldier followed shortly behind. When he got to the first wounded soldiers, he kicked him and when he realised that he was still alive, he ordered the soldier to shoot. The soldier shot him and martyred our wounded soldier. The next wounded soldier was an innocent teenager whom the officer kicked in the face. He then ordered the soldier to shoot, but the soldier refused to shoot. The officer shouted at him in front of us, but the soldier stepped back and wasn't willing to shoot! The officer withdrew his Colt pistol and shot the soldier in the face. The Iraqi soldier fell beside our martyrs onto the floor. The Iraqi officer rushed out the trench and ordered his soldiers to open fire.

Minutes later, the Iraqi soldiers left under the impression that everyone in the trench had been martyred. The sound of gunfire wasn't heard anymore and as the sun set, silence had once again descended upon Fakkeh.

A few soldiers and I had remained alive by hiding amongst the martyrs. We got up and looked around. There was no one around. Most of those who were still alive were wounded. We started our journey back in complete darkness and we reached our troops before sunrise.

CAPTIVITY

Narrator: Amir Monjar

A week had passed since we heard that Ibrahim had been lost at war. I went to the mosque before Dhuhr. Ja'far Jangravi was also there. He was grief-stricken. No one could believe it. Mostafa also came and we were talking about Ibrahim. Suddenly, Mohammad Agha Tarashkar came to us and asked, "Guys, do you know anybody by the name of Ibrahim Hadi?" We all went silent and looked at each other with surprise. We went closer, and we asked, "What happened?! What are you talking about?!" The poor man was shocked and replied, "Nothing, my brother-in-law has been lost at war for a few months, so I listen to Radio Baghdad every night at midnight. Iraq announces the names of the captives at midnight. Last night as I was listening, the radio host who was speaking Farsi suddenly cut his programme short and started playing music. He then announced gleefully, 'In this operation, Ibrahim Hadi, one of the Iranian commanders on the western line, has been taken captive by our forces.'" We were all overjoyed that Ibrahim was still alive to the extent that we did not know how to express our joy. I quickly went to my other friends. Haj Ali Sadiqi wrote a letter to the Red Cross and Reza Houryar went to Ibrahim's house to inform his brother. Everyone was ecstatic to hear that he was still alive.

A while later, we got a letter from the Red Cross. It read, "I am Ibrahim Hadi, a fifteen-year-old soldier from Najafabad, Isfahan. I think you have mistaken me for one of the commanders in the west of the country like the Iraqis!." Even though the reply had arrived, many of our friends were waiting for Ibrahim to come back until the prisoners were released. Whenever Ibrahim's name was mentioned in a majlis, they would recite about the calamities that befell Lady Fatimah (a) and everyone would cry.

SEPARATION

Narrator: Abbas Hadi

A month passed since Ibrahim was lost at war and none of his friends were seen to be happy. Whenever we met up, we would talk about Ibrahim and cry. We went to visit one of our friends in the hospital. Reza Goudini was also there. When Reza saw me, it was as if I opened the wounds of his heart again. He started weeping loudly and said, "Guys, a world without Ibrahim is not worth living in for me. I assure you that I will be martyred in the next operation!" Another said, "We never understood who Ibrahim really was. He was a sincere servant of Allah. He came for a short while and lived among us so that we could understand what servitude to Allah is." Another stated, "Ibrahim was a complete and true champion; a mystical champion!"

Five months passed since Ibrahim's martyrdom. Whenever our mother would ask why Ibrahim wouldn't come on leave, we would make an excuse to change the subject. We would say, "He is on an operation," or "He cannot come right now." We would always say one thing or another until one day, our mother walked into the room, sat in front of Ibrahim's photo and started crying. I went closer and asked her what had happened, and she replied, "I can smell Ibrahim! Ibrahim is in the room right now! He's right here!" When she stopped crying, she said, "I am sure that Ibrahim has been martyred." She continued, "Last time, Ibrahim had changed a lot. No matter how much I insisted for him to get married, he would tell me, 'No mum, I'm sure that I'm not going to return. I don't want there to be tear-filled eyes waiting for me at home!'"

A few days later, she stood in front of Ibrahim's photo and started crying again. Eventually, we had to bring our uncle to tell our mother the truth. That day, our mother's health deteriorated.

Her heart problems worsened, and we had to take her into CCU.

For the next few years, whenever we would take our mother to Behesht-e Zahra, she would prefer to sit in the 44th Sector next to the graves of the anonymous martyrs, in memory of Ibrahim. Even though she would cry a lot for him there, she would open the locks of her heart and speak with the martyrs to her heart's content.

SEARCHING FOR THE MARTYRS

Narrators: Saeed Qasemi, **Second narrator:** Ibrahim's sister

In 1990, the freed prisoners returned to their homeland. Some were still waiting for Ibrahim to return (two freed prisoners had the name Ibrahim Hadi) but to no avail. The year after, some of Ibrahim's friends went to Fakkeh to visit the war regions. On this journey, they found the bodies of several martyrs and sent them back to Tehran. A few days later, we went to visit the families of the martyrs. The mother of a martyr asked me, "Do you know where my son was martyred?" I replied, "Yes, we were together at the time." She asked, "Now that the war has ended, could you find his body and bring it back?" I started pondering over the words of this mother.

The next day, I spoke to some of the commanders and veterans. We agreed to start searching for the bodies of our martyred friends. A while later, we went to Fakkeh with a few friends. After beginning the new search, the bodies of three hundred martyrs were discovered including the son of that mother. After that, a group named 'Searching for Martyrs' was established, and they started their work in different spots along the border. The love of the oppressed martyrs of Fakkeh fuelled an extensive search in Fakkeh despite the many difficulties and dangers of the work. Many members of the group who were Ibrahim's friends would say,

"The founder of this group is Ibrahim Hadi. After every operation, he would search for the bodies of the martyrs."

Five years after the end of the war and after great difficulty, they started working on the trench known as the Kumayl Trench. The bodies of the martyrs were found one after the other. At the end of the trench, quite a few martyrs were found gathered. We were able to withdraw the martyrs from the trench with great ease, but there was no trace of Ibrahim!

Ali Mahmoudvand was the director of the group. In Operation Before the Dawn, he was besieged by the enemy in the Kumayl trench for five days. Ali felt indebted to Ibrahim and would say, "No one knows about the oppression of Fakkeh or how many of our oppressed soldiers are in these trenches. The soil of Fakkeh bears the scent of oppression from Karbala."

One day whilst searching, the body of a martyr was found. We found a booklet in the equipment he had with him which was still legible despite years of ageing. On the final page of the booklet, it was written, "Today is the fifth day of besiegement. We have rationed food and water. The martyrs are laid beside one another at the end of the trench. The martyrs are not thirsty anymore. May I be the sacrifice of your dry lips, oh son of Zahra[113] (a)!" When we read this notebook, we were overwhelmed and searched even more. There was still no trace of Ibrahim's body even though we had found the majority of the martyrs in the region.

A while later, one of Ibrahim's friends came to Fakkeh to visit. He said whilst he was narrating memories, "Don't look for Ibrahim too much! He wanted to be lost at war. I doubt you will find his body. Ibrahim will stay in Fakkeh to act as a light for those seeking guidance!"

---

113   Imam Husayn (a)

Towards the end of the '90s, another search began in Fakkeh. Once again, many martyrs were withdrawn from the trench, but almost all of them were unknown. It was in this search where Ali Mahmoudvand and, a short while later, Majeed Pazouki were also martyred.[114]

The bodies of the unknown martyrs were sent to the headquarters of the 'Searching for Martyrs' Group. They decided that after a glorious funeral in every city of the country, the five martyrs would be buried in different locations of the country during the days leading up to the martyrdom of Lady Fatimah (a). The night before the funeral in Tehran, I saw Ibrahim in my dream. He stopped outside our house on his motorcycle and said cheerfully while waving at me, "I have also come back!" In another dream, I saw the funeral procession of the martyrs. One of the coffins of the martyrs moved a little on the truck and Ibrahim came out and smiled at us with his beautiful face.

The next day, the grateful people of this country came to see the martyrs off and a magnificent funeral was held. After this, the martyrs were sent to different cities to be laid to rest. I think Ibrahim came back with the caravan of martyrs on the martyrdom anniversary of Lady Fatimah (a) to wipe the dust of ignorance from our faces. For this reason, I remember Ibrahim whenever I visit the graves of the anonymous martyrs and I recite a Fatihah for the Ibrahims of our nation.

PRESENCE

In 1997, a mural of Ibrahim's face was drawn underneath the bridge overlooking Shaheed Mohallati Highway. This was a great milestone for us in our neighbourhood. In the last few days of

---

[114] The mines in the war regions hadn't been deactivated, so these people were martyred by those mines

compiling this book, I went to the Sayyid and asked, "Agha Sayyid, I heard that you are the one who drew the mural of Shaheed Hadi, is this true?" He said yes and asked why to which I replied, "No reason, I just wanted to thank you. Ibrahim's presence will still be in the neighbourhood with this mural." He told me, "I didn't know Ibrahim, neither did I want anything in return for drawing his portrait. However, after doing this, Allah has bestowed so many blessings upon me that I can't even count them for you! I have seen things from this drawing." I was awestricken and asked, "Like what, for example?" He answered, "When I painted this portrait and the Exhibition of Martyrs opened, a woman came to me one Thursday night and told me, 'Agha, these cakes have been baked for this martyr, please distribute them here.' I thought that she was one of the martyr's relatives, so I asked her, "Do you know Shaheed Hadi?" She said no and when she saw the curiosity on my face, she added, 'My house is close. I had a serious problem in my life. A few days ago, I passed by you whilst you were busy painting the mural and I thought to myself, 'Oh Allah if this martyr has a position in Your eyes, resolve my problems by this martyr's right!' I then added, 'I promise that I will also pray all of my prayers on time," and then I recited a Fatihah for this martyr who I didn't recognise.'"

The Sayyid continued, "Last year, I was finding it difficult to find a job. I had many problems. I passed by the Agha Ibrahim's portrait and noticed that the mural had become discoloured due to time. I got some scaffolding and paint and I started repairing the martyr's portrait. It was unbelievable; as soon as I finished my work on the mural, a huge project was offered to me. Most of my financial problems were resolved." He then added, "Agha, they have a great position in the eyes of Allah, and we are yet to fully recognise them. Even if you do the smallest of favours for them, Allah will multiply it manifold for you."

A man had come to the mosque and asked me where he could find Agha Ibrahim's friends. He wanted to ask them a few questions about the martyr. I asked him, "What do you need? Maybe I can help you." He said, "Nothing, I just wanted to know who Shaheed Hadi was and where his grave is." I thought a little; I didn't know what to say. I said a few moments later, "Ibrahim Hadi's body was lost at war and he doesn't have a grave, just like all martyrs lost at war. Why are you asking about this martyr?"

The man became very distressed and said, "My house is close to Shaheed Hadi's mural. I have a young daughter and she passes by the mural every day to go to school. One time, she asked me who this man was, and I explained, "These people went and fought the enemy. They didn't let the enemy attack us and then they were martyred." Since she heard this, whenever she passes by the mural, she says salaam to the portrait of Shaheed Hadi. A few nights ago, my daughter saw this martyr in her *dream*. Shaheed Hadi said to my daughter, 'My dear sister, whenever you say salaam, I reply to you. I pray for you as well because you observe the hijab properly even though you are so young.' Now, my daughter is asking who this Shaheed Hadi is and where his grave is!" My eyes welled up with tears and I didn't know what to say. All I said was, "Tell your daughter that if she wants Ibrahim to always pray for her, she should be careful about her prayers and observe her hijab properly." I then told him some stories from Ibrahim's life.

I remember I once saw a sentence written on an

announcement board, 'The relationship and friendship with the martyrs is a two-way relationship; if you side with them, they will also side with you.'

At the end of March 2009, we set off for Gilan-e Gharb to complete our research for the book. On the way, we reached the city of Eyvan. The sun was setting, and we were exhausted. We had been driving since the morning. However, we couldn't find any hotels in the city. I thought to myself, "Agha Ibrahim, we came to do your work, please sort it out yourself." At that moment, we heard the adhan of Maghrib. I thought to myself, "If Ibrahim was here, he would have gone to pray in the mosque," so we went to the mosque and prayed congregational prayers.

After prayers, a man who looked about fifty years old came up to us and said salaam respectfully. He asked if we had come from Tehran and I replied, "Yes, how did you know?" He replied, "It says it on the registration plate on your car." He then continued, "Our house is close by and everything is ready [for guests]. Would you like to come?" I said, "Thank you, but we need to leave." He insisted, "Rest for tonight and set off tomorrow." I didn't want to accept, but the caretaker of the mosque came to me and said, "This is Agha Mohammadi, one of the officials of this city. Accept his invitation." I was too tired, so I accepted, and we went together. He fed us a large dinner and welcomed us very warmly.

In the morning, we ate breakfast and then we bade farewell to him. Agha Mohammadi asked, "May I ask why you came to this city?" I replied, "We are going to Gilan-e Gharb to gather some memories of a martyr." He said with surprise, "I was one of the soldiers from Gilan-e Gharb. Which martyr?" I replied, "You won't recognise him, he came from Tehran." I proceeded to take the photo out from my bag and show it to him. He looked with wonder and exclaimed, "This is Agha Ibrahim! My father and I were Shaheed Hadi's soldiers. We were together on operations and reconnaissance operations during the first year of the war." I was looked at him with great awe. I was lost for words and choked up with tears. From the night before until morning, we were welcomed extremely warmly, and it turned out that our host was one of his friends! Agha Ibrahim, I'm grateful to you. We prayed on time in your memory and you solved our problems.

PEACE BE UPON IBRAHIM

When we decided to compile a book on Agha Ibrahim, we put all our effort into it so that we could do the best work possible with Allah's help, although we know that this compilation is only a drop from the ocean of Ibrahim's perfection and eminence. From the beginning, I was grateful to Allah for introducing me to one of His pure and sincere servants. I was grateful to Allah that He chose me for this work. During this time, I have also noticed wonderful changes in my life.

It took almost two years of effort, sixty interviews, many journeys and many edits of the text of the book to bring this to your hands. I wanted to find a title for this book which would be synonymous with Ibrahim's character and spirituality. I met with Haj Hosein Allah-Karam and asked him, "Do you have any suggestions for the title of the book?" He replied, "Adhan. Many of the soldiers recognised him by his adhan, by his wonderful adhan!" Another mentioned, "Shaheed Hesami would call him the mystic champion," but I had already chosen the title, 'The Miracle of the Adhan,' for the book.

I was thinking about it throughout the night. The Qur'an on the table beside me caught my eye, and I picked it up. I thought to myself, "O' Allah, this work was for Your sincere and anonymous servant. I want to know the Qur'an's opinion on what the title of the book should be." I then said to Allah, "Up until now, everything has been from Your blessings. I had never met Ibrahim nor was

I old enough to go to the warfront, but You loved me enough to let me compile this book. O' Allah, I neither know how to do an istikharah nor can I correctly interpret your verses, [so help me!]" I said Bismillah, read Surah Fatihah and opened the Qur'an on the table. I looked carefully at the page which I had opened. When I saw the verse at the top of the page, I went pale! I felt lightheaded and I started crying uncontrollably. At the top of the page, I saw the 109th verse of Surah Saffat which reads:

> *'Peace be to Ibrahim!' (109)*
> *Thus, do We reward the virtuous. (110)*
> *He is indeed one of Our faithful servants. (111)*

THE MARTYRS ARE ALIVE
Narrator: Mostafa Saffar Harandi and others

These are not our words. The Qur'an says that the martyrs are alive. The martyrs witness everything in this world and they understand the happenings of this world better than when they were alive as they are aware of the conditions on the other side. When we were gathering the memories for this book, we witnessed Allah's help and even help from Ibrahim himself. Many times, he would come himself and would tell us who to interview!

However, we would feel Agha Ibrahim's presence and the presence of the other martyrs more during the difficult periods in the country. We could feel this presence during the events and riots that took place after the war. In June 1999, riots broke out which brought joy to the hearts of the enemies of our country, but Allah wished for the instigators to encounter a bad end. On the first night when these riots began, nobody had any idea of what was happening. That night, I saw Shaheed Commander Boroujerdi in my dream. He had gathered all the people who attend the mosque and took them to one of Tehran's intersections. It was a lot like the time when Imam Khomeini (ra) returned to Iran on the 1st of February 1979 when he was responsible for coordinating the Imam (ra)'s schedule. I was standing with the guys from the mosque next to Brother Boroujerdi. All of a sudden, I saw Ibrahim Hadi, Javad Afrasyabi, Reza and my other martyred friends standing next to Brother Boroujerdi. I was so happy. I wanted to go to them, but I saw that Brother Boroujerdi had a piece of paper in his hands and was busy stationing the troops around Tehran like he would at the beginning of an operation. He positioned all his troops including Ibrahim in different places around the University of Tehran.

In the morning, I thought about the dream a lot. What could it mean?! I was thinking about this until my friends called me and informed me that there had been clashes at the University of Tehran and that the university had been taken by the anti-revolutionaries. When I heard this, I remembered my dream from the night before.

The riots of '99 ended quickly. On the 15th of July, the people disassociated themselves from the instigators of the riots with a great march of solidarity. That day, I saw Haj Ali Nasrollah who had come to take part in the march despite his illness. I stated, "Haj Ali, these riots were ended by the martyrs." Haj Ali turned around and replied, "What else could it be? Be sure that this was the work of the martyrs!"

WHERE ARE YOU GOING?!

Narrator: Mrs Rasouli

During the Holy Defence, I went to the warfront with my husband. He was part of the Shaheed Andarzgu Battalion and I was a medic at the Gilan-e Gharb Hospital. It was in that hospital where I saw Ibrahim Hadi for the first time. One time, he brought a few bodies of the martyrs to the hospital and said to us, "Ladies, don't come forward! The bodies of the martyrs have been severely mutilated, and we have to identify them."

After that, I heard his heavenly voice several times. He had a very beautiful voice. When he would recite duas, everyone would start crying. I noticed that the soldiers loved Ibrahim and they would always gather around him.

At the start of 1982, they went to the south and I went back to Tehran. A few years later, as I was walking down 17 Shahrivar Street, I saw a photo of Agha Ibrahim on the wall. I had no idea that he was martyred and lost at war. From then on, I pray a two-unit prayer every Thursday night in his remembrance and the remembrance of the other martyrs.

One night in 2009 during the riots, something strange happened. I had a dream in which I saw Ibrahim sitting at the top of a very green hill, and his face was shining. Behind him, I saw many beautiful trees. I then noticed that two of his friends who I also knew were at the bottom of the hill and they were struggling in quicksand. They wanted to go somewhere, but the more they struggled, the more they sank into the quicksand. Ibrahim turned to them and recited a verse of the Qur'an, "Then, where are you going!?"[115] but they didn't pay any attention to him.

I pondered upon this dream a lot the next day. What could this dream mean?! My son came home from university. He came straight up to me excitedly and said, "Mum, I got you a gift." He took a book out of his bag and said, "Shaheed Ibrahim Hadi's book has been printed!" When I saw the front cover, my face went pale. My son became concerned and asked, "Mum, what happened? I thought you'd be happy." I came closer and said, "Let me see this book." I had seen the same scene on the cover in my dream the night before and I had seen Ibrahim in that state. From then on, I started studying the book.

When I realised that my dream had a true meaning, I got my

---

115   Surah Takweer: 26

husband to contact one of the soldiers in that period. We asked him if he knew anything about those two people who I had seen in my dream. After some research, I found out that those two people were instigators of the riots and had turned against the Leader of the Islamic Revolution despite their years of military service and experience on the warfront. Even though a dream is not counted as Islamic evidence, I considered it my duty to ring them and inform them of the dream. All thanks due to Allah, this dream had an effect and Ibrahim once again became the guide of his friends.

THE MEMORIAL GRAVESTONE
Narrator: The martyr's sister

After Ibrahim, there was no joy in my life. Ibrahim was my whole life. I was very attached to him. Not only was he our older brother, but he was also our trainer. He spoke to me many times about the hijab and he would say, "The veil is a souvenir from Lady Fatimah (a). A woman's faith is complete once she observes hijab to its perfection." Whenever we wanted to leave the house or we were invited somewhere, he would advise us on how to act with non-mahrams. However, he would never ban us or order us to do anything. Ibrahim would train us through advice.

He would wake us up for Fajr with jokes and laughter, and he would say, "Prayers should only be prayed at the beginning of its time and in congregation." He would always advise his friends to recite the adhan and he would tell them, "Whenever you hear the adhan, stop even if you are riding your motorcycle and call your Lord with a loud voice and recite the adhan."

When Ibrahim was wounded and came home on leave, we would be glad on one hand and upset on the other. We were upset since he was wounded and glad that we could spend more time with him. I remember well that some of his friends came to visit him and Ibrahim started reciting a poem that I think he wrote himself:

> *"Even if the whole world turns against us,*
> *Even if with blades they shed my blood,*
> *Even if with blood they drench my body,*
> *Even if from my body they separate my head,*
> *Even if blood and fire destroy my body,*
> *I will never cross the red line of my leader!"*

I heard him say often, "We only go to the warfront to be martyred. Otherwise, we wouldn't like it at all!" He would say to his friends, "Always say that you will give your life for Islam and the Revolution until your last moment. If Allah wills and we pass all our tests, only then will we be martyred. Until then, we must fight in His way." He would say, "We must train this body of ours so much and be active in Allah's way so much so that when He sees fit, He will allow us to be martyred. However, it is possible that the blessing of martyrdom may be taken away from us due to inappropriate conduct."

Many years passed since Ibrahim's martyrdom. No one could imagine what his loss had put our family through. The news knocked our mother off her feet.

In 2011, I heard that a memorial gravestone for Ibrahim was going to be built over a grave of one of the anonymous martyrs in Behesht-e Zahra. Ibrahim loved being unknown and now, they were building a memorial gravestone for him above the grave of an anonymous martyr. In reality, this unknown martyr was being honoured by Ibrahim.

The first time I visited his memorial, I felt shivers down my spine. My face went pale and I looked around with surprise. A few of our relatives were in a similar state to me. We all remembered what had happened thirty years ago in this very spot. Right after the operation in which Khorramshahr was liberated, my mother's cousin Shaheed Hasan Serajiyan was martyred. At that time, Ibrahim was injured and would walk with a crutch, but he still came to Behesht-e Zahra to pay his respects. When they buried Hasan, Ibrahim went forward and said, "Good for you, Hasan, what a great place you have! Sector 26, next to the main road. Whoever passes by here will read Fatihah for you and will remember you!" He then added, "I should also come to you. Pray that I can also come here!" He then struck the ground and pointed at a grave a few graves down from Hasan's grave with his crutch. A few years later, an unknown martyr was buried in the exact same place he had shown us. Even stranger, Ibrahim's memorial gravestone was placed on his grave in the very same place he wanted to be buried!

ENDNOTES

This beloved martyr has led to some amazing things happening, from curing a cancer patient in Yazd to a bad university student who somehow became familiar with Ibrahim and changed his life. Also, there was a youth who, wherever he went to propose, he would be rejected. He prayed to Allah through Shaheed Hadi and in the last house that he went for proposal, Ibrahim's photo was the decoration piece and they had also asked Allah through Shaheed Hadi for everything to go smoothly.

In these few years, there has not even been a day where we have forgotten him. All our lives were changed by him. Ibrahim made the way smooth so that, with Allah's help, thirty other books were written about the martyrs and were printed. With the route that Ibrahim had shown us, tens of other martyrs lost at war were introduced to us and this country.

Maybe on the first day, we didn't think it would turn out like this, but our dear Ibrahim, the role model of sincerity and servitude, has become the role model of manners for people even in other countries and nations. A few people from Kashmir came and asked permission to translate this book into Urdu and publish it in India and Pakistan. They were saying that this person is the best of role models and this was done in February 2013. Yes, we went after the words of the late Shaykh Hosein Zahed to see if they were true, and with Allah's help, these words were confirmed. Ibrahim is a role model for manners for every human being who wants to learn how to live properly.

www.ingramcontent.com/pod-product-compliance
Lightning Source LLC
Chambersburg PA
CBHW060603080526
44585CB00013B/672